MESSAGE OF BIBLICAL SPIRITUALITY
Editorial Director: Carolyn Osiek, RSCJ

Volume 7

The Old Testament Short Story

Explorations into Narrative Spirituality

Carmel McCarthy, RSM *& William Riley*

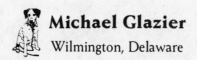

Michael Glazier
Wilmington, Delaware

ABOUT THE AUTHORS

Carmel McCarthy, RSM lectures in Scripture at Carysfort College of Education, Dublin and in the Department of Semitic Languages at University College, Dublin. She is on the board for *Scripture in Church,* and holds a doctorate from the University of Fribourg, Switzerland. She has published a detailed study of the *Tiqqune Sopherim* (Scribal Emendations) to the Masoretic Text of the Old Testament.

William Riley studied biblical theology at the Angelicum University in Rome. He now lectures in Scripture at the Mater Dei Institute of Education, Dublin. He is the author of *The Bible Study Group: An Owner's Manual* and *The Tale of Two Testaments.*

First published in 1986 by Michael Glazier, Inc. 1935 West Fourth Street, Wilmington, Delaware, 19805. ©1986 by Michael Glazier, Inc. All rights reserved. Library of Congress Catalog Card Number: 86-45325. International Standard Book Numbers: *Message of Biblical Spirituality* series: 0-89453-550-1, cloth; 0-89453-566-8, paper. THE OLD TESTAMENT SHORT STORY: 0-89453-577-9, cloth; 0-89453-573-0, paper. Typography by Dick Smith. Cover design by Florence Bern. Printed in the United States of America.

TABLE OF CONTENTS

93788

EDITOR'S PREFACE

One of the characteristics of church life today is a revived interest in spirituality. There is a growing list of resources in this area, yet the need for more is not exhausted. People are yearning for guidance in living an integrated life of faith in which belief, attitude, affections, prayer, and action form a cohesive unity which gives meaning to their lives.

The biblical tradition is a rich resource for the variety of ways in which people have heard God's call to live a life of faith and fidelity. In each of the biblical books we have a witness to the initiative of God in human history and to the attempts of people not so different from ourselves to respond to the revelation of God's love and care.

The fifteen volumes in the *Message of Biblical Spirituality* series aim to provide ready access to the treasury of biblical faith. Modern social science has made us aware of how the particular way in which one views reality conditions the ways in which one will interpret experience and life itself. Each volume in this series is an attempt to retell and interpret the biblical story from within the faith perspective that originally formed it. Each seeks to portray what it is like to see God, the world, and oneself from a particular point of view and to search for ways to respond faithfully to that vision. We who are citizens of our twentieth century world cannot be people of the ancient biblical world, but we can grow closer to their experience and their faith and thus closer to God, through the living Word of God which is the Bible.

The series includes an international group of authors representing England, Ireland, Canada, and the United States, but whose life experience has included first-hand knowledge of many other countries. All are proven scholars and committed believers whose faith is as important to them as their scholarship. Each acts as interpreter of one part of the biblical tradition in order to enable its spiritual vitality to be passed on to others. It is our hope that through their labor the reader will be able to enter more deeply into the life of faith, hope, and love through a fuller understanding of and appreciation for the biblical Word as handed down to us by God's faithful witnesses, the biblical authors themselves.

Carolyn Osiek, RSCJ
Associate Professor of New Testament Studies
Catholic Theological Union, Chicago

INTRODUCTION

Much emphasis has been placed in recent years on the study of narrative, not only in the field of literature, as one might expect, but also in the field of anthropology and folklore. It was a natural development that this interest would eventually find its way into biblical studies first, and then into the wider theological conversation.

This volume is, essentially, an exploration of narrative and of the significant fact that the Jewish and Christian communities have persisted over the centuries in telling stories which they reverence as the Word of God. The first two chapters give a general approach to story with a particular emphasis on biblical narrative. The next five chapters utilise this approach in various ways to explore the five books of the Catholic canon which consist of self-contained and unified narrative; we have termed these books "The Old Testament Short Story" and acknowledge the anachronism. These chapters are not intended to be a comprehensive treatment of the books examined; our only concern is to explore them as stories, created by, and still having continued existence in, the community of faith. A final chapter isolates some of the authors' reflections on the place and message of story in the Christian life. There is an appendix which deals more specifically with the historical background which these books invoke and in which they were formed; this will be of particular interest to those who are interested in the relationship of these narratives and their composition to the historical events of the ancient world. Readers who feel less than familiar with the historical background of the individual books might wish to read the relevant section of this appendix before examining the analysis offered in the main body of this volume.

We wish to express our gratitude to those who offered their comments on aspects of the material presented in this book; this would include many of our colleagues in Our Lady of Mercy College of Education, Carysfort, the Mater Dei Institute of Education, the Department of Semitic Languages in University College Dublin, and the Irish Biblical Association. Particularly deserving of mention in this context are Dr. Brendan McDonnell of the Mater Dei Institute and Sr. Regina Durkan, President of Our Lady of Mercy College of Education, both of whom read the manuscript and offered valued suggestions.

The chapters on Ruth, Esther and Judith, as well as the Appendix, are largely the work of Carmel McCarthy; responsibility for the two opening chapters on narrative and the concluding chapter, as well as the chapters on Jonah and Tobit, belongs chiefly to William Riley.

Carmel McCarthy, RSM
William Riley

Our Lady of Mercy College of Education
Carysfort Park,
Blackrock, Co Dublin.

1

WHY TELL THE OLD, OLD STORY?

Recent years have witnessed a new approach to the interpretation of Scripture. This should hardly be surprising, since many ages have brought their particular insights to the work of discovering the meaning of God's Word, forging new tools with which to mine Scripture's treasures. Our age is at present trying to rediscover the literary characteristics and qualities to be found in the biblical books, and it is from this quest that the present volume on the narrative of the Bible results.

In the past — and among some Christians today — the only important fact to know when interpreting Scripture was that the Bible is the Word of God. For such readers, this meant that everything in the Bible is true (and "true" in any sense that you care to think of). Every statement, every detail must be historical and accurate; each phrase (whether in context or out of context, I know not — God knows) might contain doctrines essential to orthodoxy. This approach has generated much genuine love of Scripture and deep biblical spirituality; but it has also spawned monsters: expeditions to discover

Noah's ark, dates for the Second Coming calculated from the Apocalypse and Daniel, cults and sects and fanaticism of every kind. While the basic insight of this approach is essential for any Christian study of Scripture, in many cases its develop-- ment has obviously gone astray.

Another approach — much more associated with the realms of biblical scholarship — concentrates on Scripture as a human document, temporarily setting aside its claim to be a divine document as well. This method — or more accurately, this assorted set of scholarly tools — is often referred to as the "historical-critical method." It has given us great insights into the meaning of Scripture through its insistence on putting each passage back into its original setting before the process of interpretation begins. Unfortunately, its real fame is often limited to its ability to place question marks over the historic- ity of events narrated in the Bible. And many believers find it especially painful that these question marks seem to congregate around the gospel accounts of the life of Jesus. Many people would agree with the man who reacted to a scholar's explana- tion of a gospel text by saying, "The exegetes have taken my Lord and I don't know where they have laid him." Oftentimes the writings of Scripture seem to be regarded simply as evi- dence of dubious trust-worthiness to past events: it is in those reconstructed events, many assume, that the real revelation of God is to be found.

The literary approach to the Bible has largely grown out of the historical-critical workings. The rediscovery of the human- ity of the documents with its new emphasis on the intentions of the authors and the setting of the text's original use had to lead, eventually, to the realisation that the religious purposes of these writings were achieved more according to the norms of poetics than of historiography. The literary approach depends on the continuing insights of the historical-critical school; indeed, it would be misleading to draw too black a line between the two approaches. The literary approach also listens to what is happening in the study of secular literature and in the study of language generally to discover how stories and poems work and how best to interpret them. The literary approach shares the conviction that the Bible is the Word of God, offering to humanity a unique and transforming vision cloaked in all of the delights and fascinating intricacies of human speech.

The literary approach has produced much worthy material, written from many different backgrounds, at different levels of technicality, reflecting different schools of literary theory. It is hardly the purpose of a volume such as this to reflect comprehensively all that is being written in this developing field. Instead, in this chapter and the next, we will discuss the nature and mechanics of biblical storytelling and how the biblical story forms the Christian vision. In consequent chapters, we will deal more specifically with five self-contained narratives of the Old Testament — the type of writing which would be termed a short story if produced today.

The Problem of Interpreting

Interpreters work in an ancient profession. The saga of Joseph in the book of Genesis mentions interpreters in the Egyptian court of the second millennium B.C. (Gen. 42:23), so they are not simply the by-product of multinational companies and modern communications. The process of interpreting seems simple enough: X makes a statement, intended for Y, but Y does not understand the language that X uses; so Z, who can communicate in both the language of X and the language of Y, translates the statement which X has made into Y's language. And the process goes back and forth until the conversation is complete.

This is obviously closer to the task of the biblical translator than to that of the biblical interpreter; yet there is common ground between the purely linguistic interpreter and the exegetical interpreter. A message is expressed through a medium which does not fully (nor perhaps even partially) communicate the message to the recipient. Another process is invoked to place that message into a medium which will better communicate it. The process of interpretation, by necessity, means removing the message from its original medium into a medium for which it was not originally intended. In the case of the linguistic interpreter, this process is from like to like, i.e. from one language to another; in the case of the biblical interpreter, the process is from unlike to unlike, e.g. from a song for cantor, choir and dancers to a fifteen page essay with footnotes and bibliography, from an assault upon the ears and eyes which sets feet tapping to an assault upon the intellect which sets the eyelids drooping. The process of biblical interpretation (or indeed of any interpretation), no matter how carefully done, is a matter of uprooting a message from the ground in which it lives. Biblical spirituality tries to transplant these living organisms into fertile ground in which they can continue to thrive; it is not interested in collecting dead specimens.

We should examine briefly the ground in which our seedlings are growing before we touch them at all. Since our concern is the biblical story, then we can be certain that there are at least three elements involved: (1) the storyteller; (2) the story; (3) the audience. Each of these has some bearing on the message of the piece under consideration. The storyteller determines the original message and the form in which that message is to be communicated; he or she has certain projections as to the effects which the story will have, but no absolute control over these effects. The story which is produced is the creation of the storyteller, yet also exists as a separate entity; once formed and communicated, its existence and impact is no longer totally dependent upon the existence or intentions of the storyteller. The (original) audience is also an important factor in determining the meaning of the message, for its reaction tells us what impact the message actually has — which can be at variance with the impact intended by the author. Of these three elements, the only one which we possess in the case of most biblical narratives is the second, the text of the story itself. From this, and from the scraps of related information available to us, we must make a tentative reconstruction of the author's purpose and of the audience's reaction; through this process, we hopefully can locate ourselves as a fourth element, the audience unforeseen by the original author for whom the message still has impact and importance. If this can be done successfully, then the message is no longer uprooted but transplanted as a living communication.

Story as Experiment

The very word experiment conjures up images of white coats, white rats and laboratory conditions. The experimenter knows what he or she is at, but does not necessarily know the result. An experiment may be intended to discover the unknown, but it is no haphazard affair. The materials are carefully selected, measured, the process is timed, the result painstakingly noted.

Perhaps the type of experimentations in which the story-teller indulges might be better compared to a child playing with blocks than to the research scientist at work. The child piles and structures the components, allowing gravity to decide upon the success of the experiment. The rules are simple: staying up is a success; falling down is a failure.

In the story-experiment, the storyteller attempts to present a message through a viable portrayal of reality and its workings. Although the story never exactly represents the experience of the audience, it is presenting elements of reality in such a way as to help the audience order their own experience of reality meaningfully. The audience of the story judge the success of the experiment, measuring their own experience of life against the story and the story against their experience of life. The successful story-experiment is the one which either presents a message which reveals a truth hidden until the telling of the story, or which confirms a truth already accepted by the audience, or which establishes its message as a possibility to be reckoned with — even though the story has not succeeded in totally convincing the audience. The unsuccessful story-experiment leaves the audience with the feeling that, no, reality is not like this; the story may have been well told and enter-taining, but it will only satisfy the hearer if it succeeds in expanding or enriching or confirming or altering the previously held world-view.

All of this leads directly to the discussion of biblical stories as true. To the modern mind, the only way that a story can claim to be true is if all of the details and events related in it have actually taken place in the past. No one could deny that this attitude has a certain logic behind it: the only way in which the story-experiment can be judged to be valid is if it has been played out in life, its machinations noted, its results sifted and analysed, the important findings published. Forget the child and building blocks; here we're talking *science*.

Such an attitude finds it convenient to overlook the fact that historical stories are also creations of human talent, dependent for their existence on the storyteller as much as on the happening. The story of Jack the Ripper is a true story — it happened, the details are available, the mystery is still unsolved. But the family breakfast this morning also happened, as did the rainfall yesterday, as did a thousand other things dramatic and commonplace, which will never be told as true stories, for they lack the storyteller. The teller of the true story does possess a slightly different talent to the story-maker: one pieces together blocks of reality to make a new creation; the other chips away parts of reality to sculpt according to the teller's creative insights. But, in the end, both produce artifacts which serve the same functions in human society.

Instead of looking for the truth of the story in the factuality of the events it narrates, one could be equally justified in seeing its worth in the persistence of its telling. Stories which are told and retold, even when presented in different guises, obviously strike a note of truth in the audience; the certain verdict of validity has been passed when a hearer of the story becomes the story's teller. In some respects, the most worthwhile stories of a society are not the highly crafted works of its literary geniuses, but the humble oral tradition. Such stories are perhaps primitive, often unartistic, but they persist because of their accurate reflection of the society's hopes, fears and values.

Such an evaluation of story's truth is necessarily subjective; people outside of the narrating society may well reject the story since they do not share in the vision which the story enshrines. But stories contain an objective truth as well: they state accurately the attitudes of the society which has formed and transmitted the story in its tradition. To take the traditional story of George Washington and the cherry tree as an example, one might quibble with the objective fact which seems to be enshrined in the story — but one cannot quibble with the idea that, to the American traditional consciousness, it is important that this central figure of America's national origins was thoroughly upright and trustworthy. The objective truth of story is to be found in what it reveals about those who tell the story and those who validate it.

Biblical Story as Traditional Narrative

When we speak of biblical story, we are speaking of the traditional stories of a society. Sometimes it is a society in our normal use of the term, for instance, the Israelite tribes which carried on the stories of Abraham, Isaac and Jacob. But our interest in these stories — particularly our interest in the spiritual worth of these stories — is as members of this society in a wider sense; for we are part of the community of faith which continues to validate and transmit these stories as part of its tradition. In this context, it might become somewhat clearer that we have often been mistaken in our search for the objective value of the biblical stories: we have too often been concerned with what actually happened and what did not happen. Such matters — which ultimately lie beyond the realm of conclusive proof and within the realm of continual debate — have nothing to do with the objective truth of these narratives as story; their objective truth lies in what they have to say about the vision and values of the society which originally told these stories and which we continue to form as a community of believers. It is the latter consideration which will point the way to the religious truth of these stories.

We have long accepted that non-historical stories form an important part of the Christian tradition. The parables of Jesus are the obvious example of tales which no one was meant to take as factual reporting of events. Did it make any difference whether a man actually *did* go down from Jerusalem to Jericho and fall among thieves? Does the lesson gain anything if it is discovered someday that things actually happened as related in Luke 10? But while believers have accepted that such important narratives within their tradition have no reality in history, they begin to panic when the scholar tells them that the Red Sea may not have stood up like walls of water or Jonah may have had no experiences in the belly of a fish. And one may well question why the validity of a patently non-historical story can be accepted without difficulty while the slightest doubt about the historicity of a different (and often less central) biblical story brings the entire volume into disrepute.

We do an injustice to the role of the audience if we limit it to listening. The audience must perform one more activity before the story-experiment can be performed; this activity is often referred to, in the words of Coleridge, as the *suspension of disbelief,* the action by which the audience lowers itself into the story world to observe and to judge. If at any time within the telling of the story, the audience decides that the story must invoke disbelief, then the experiment is aborted and the story is not experienced. If disbelief is successfully kept at bay throughout the story, then the message of the story has been experienced and can be judged according to the experience.

The "true" story has suspension of disbelief as an inbuilt feature; the patently fictional story must beg for suspension of disbelief at the audience's good pleasure. In the case of biblical stories, we have traditionally given all biblical stories the full benefit of our suspension of disbelief gladly; but with different presuppositions: stories like the parables have been given it as fictional stories, but stories like Jonah and the fish have been given it on the assumption that the events actually happened. When that assumption is challenged, then the audience feels somewhat foolish, taken in by a clever narrative trick. The story is no longer as trustworthy as it seemed, and the visions it presents are now opened to a harsher questioning.

When a person assumes a literalist position in biblical matters, it is an admission that the suspension of disbelief is only possible for that person when there is no possibility of disbelief. Such an outlook is blinkered to the point of blindness. It only has credibility if the person involved never reads fiction, watches films or tells jokes, for the suspension of disbelief is required by any and all of these activities.

The religious truth of a biblical story lies in the vision and values which the story is attempting to enshrine and which the community of faith validates by its continued transmission and use of these stories. The modern mentality might have suggested to the ancient story-formers that religious truth could have been enshrined more succinctly and more effectively in a series of propositions: God is good; justice is required for a stable society; the divine plan encompasses even human suffering. But the ancients were more appreciative of the real power of story-telling; they were unhindered by the modern sophisms which distract us from narrative's functions and worth.

Story as Vehicle of Truth

The phrase "true story" generally only conveys one image: a story which is dependent on history for its characters and .events. This limits the truth of a story to its objectivity, whether the events would have existed without the story being told. Yet story's real purpose and achievement is in conveying subjective truth, truth which is meaningful to the life of the teller and of the audience. As soon as a factual story is told, it, too, enters this realm. If someone tells you the story of what happened to him when he bought the used car and how he discovered that its extensive rust was covered with a thin cosmetic layer of paint, it is a warning to you which you will carry with you if ever you make a similar investment. The story may have been objectively true, but you have embraced it now as part of your own experience; you have made its truth subjective. The same would be true even if the storyteller were fabricating a tale unbeknownst to yourself; your acceptance of its subjective truth would be the same.

The function of story, then, is to convey the truth perceived, believed, or experienced by the teller into the awareness of the audience. Both storyteller and audience may be unaware of how this takes place, and all but students of narrative will be largely unaware of the various innuendoes which have found their home in a particular tale; but the message of the story will generally be conveyed more effectively than logical argument could hope to achieve. An excellent example of this is to be found in the story of the Good Samaritan already referred to. The setting in Luke's gospel is that of an expert in the Torah arguing with Jesus about the meaning of Lv 19:18, "You shall love your neighbour as yourself." Like many legal arguments (and Luke specifically uses the term lawyer for the man with whom Jesus is discussing the mattter,) this one centres on an important term in the Law and the implications of that term. One need go no further than Mt 5:43 to show that, to many in Jesus' day, the term neighbour implied only a fellow-Israelite. Jesus wanted to extend this narrow way of thinking. He could have argued with syllogisms and common usages, scholarly opinions or the findings of the latest research. Instead, he told a story about a man in trouble, two people who observed the legal niceties (and did nothing) and the man who flouted both the legal niceties and his cultural tradition to take care of someone in trouble. The lawyer could not escape the point of the story, although there is no guarantee that the point became part of his own world-view. The story certainly gave its message a foot in the door even if the message never received a hearty welcome.

Stories as Well-Baited Traps

How does story begin to open ears which are determined to remain closed to it? The ensnaring mechanisms of story are manifold, but three are worthy of special comment.

The first, and most innocuous, is the technique of enchantment. Granted, this is not appreciably utilised in every story. The storyteller can create a world of delights and wonders which exist only through the story and which break into reality through the story's telling. The gaps are found in reality's harsh boundary and an escape is made by both storyteller and audience. Through listening to a story, the old become nimble, the unattractive blossom into beauty, the unloved venture forth on adventures of high romance. Like a holiday in exotic lands, story is broadening. What more traditional forms of narrative accomplished with words, cinematic storytelling now attempts with sets and costumes and special effects; yet the same goal of enchantment underlies both the ancient and modern techniques.

A second, and more sinister, mechanism of story is its use of fear. Nearly every story ever told deals — at least obliquely — with the reality of human fear, and many genres of fiction have its icy presence at the core: the ghost story, the terror story, the spy thriller, the murder mystery, the catastrophe novel. Once introduced into a narrative's fabric, fear is either overcome or justified by the tragedy in which it results. This, in turn, points to two types of story: those which intend to reassure the hearer and those which seek to warn the hearer. These functions are a matter which will receive further comment in the second chapter.

The third mechanism of story which ensnares the audience is its use of characters. Whether historical or fictional, the characters assume a reality for the audience at least for the duration of the storytelling. The listener relates to these characters, liking some, despising others. And, as the following example illustrates, it is largely through these characters — and the audience's reaction to them — that story can function.

> Yahweh sent Nathan to David. He came to him and told him,
> "There were two men in the one city; one was rich and one
> was poor.

"The rich man had flocks and herds in abundance, and the poor man had nothing at all, just a single tiny ewe lamb which he possessed and which grew up with him and his children. She would eat from his bit of food and drink from his cup and lie in his bosom — she was like a daughter to him.

"A traveller came to the rich man, but the rich man spared his own herds and flocks. He would not take from them to make a meal for his visitor. But he took the poor man's ewe lamb and did her for the man who had come to him."

David's anger really flared against that man, and he said to Nathan, "By the living Yahweh, the man that did this deserves to die! He will return that ewe lamb fourfold, because he did this and had no pity."

Then Nathan said to David, "You yourself are the man!" (2 Sam 12:1-7)

This highly polished literary gem illustrates the most important element in the audience's involvement with a narrative: the identification which the hearer or listener makes with one of the characters in the story. Obviously, King David listened to Nathan's narrative with tears in his eyes, the former shepherd mustering all of his sympathy and rage for the sake of this poor man who loved his little lamb. The story had drawn David into its trap; Nathan sprang the trap by revealing to David that he had identified with the wrong character in the tale: David was the villain, the man without compassion. And the story which David had obviously taken as an historical one is shown to be non-historical, but true, with all of the punch of subjective truth hitting home.

The characters are the element of the story which makes it dawn upon the hearer, "This story is about ME!" — or at least "This story *could* be about me." Such an awareness is an admission that the story-experiment has a valid basis, that this is the way in which reality can operate. But rather than leaving the truth expressed at an abstract level, story exposes it, through character identification, in all of its subjective glory. Truth becomes personalised, meaning becomes tangible, narrative becomes experience.

Audience Reaction, Passive and Active

The final stage of the story-experiment, putting everything together to see if it works, is really to be found in the reaction of the audience. This reaction is never completely within the control of the storyteller, of course, and will be different for the different members of the audience. The more complex the story, the more complex the range of reactions; often people will disagree over what a particular story is *about*, let alone over what their reaction to the perceived message should be. If the parable of the vineyard in Mark's gospel (Mk 12:1-11) might be taken as an example of a relatively simple story in this context, the note which Mark appends to the parable demonstrates that even this simple story carries more than one message.

> They wanted to arrest him, but feared the crowd, because they knew that he had told the parable against them; so they left him and went away. (Mk 12:12)

The chief priests and scribes obviously heard in this parable a condemnation of their response to the message that God had sent them through the prophets and through Jesus, with the warning that the vineyard of Israel would be removed from their control. However, the Christian reader of this parable is more likely to see the sonship of Jesus and the narrative prediction of the cross as the more important emphasis of these few sentences. Different audiences, different reactions; yet if both are the product of listening to the story on its own terms (not importing foreign presuppositions into the hearing nor misunderstanding its terms of reference), then both are worthy parts of the story-experiment and one must include both in the list of findings.

With traditional stories (and most biblical stories fit into this category), the audience reaction is often worked back into the fabric of the story itself. One way in which this is done is demonstrated by the verse from Mark quoted above; it is no longer possible for the evangelist simply to relate the parable that has come to him in the tradition, for the reaction of part of the audience extends and interprets the story and must also be recorded. The same could be said about Nathan's parable in the Second Book of Samuel. But the audience reaction has also affected the way in which the story itself is told and retold. We hear of strange experiences (you know, the type that never has happened to the teller, but to a second cousin of a friend of his) and eventually pass them on ourselves, but some small detail of place or age slips in, nearly unknown to ourselves. We repeat a joke that we heard a few weeks back, but never verbatim; sometimes we are even lucky not to have jeopardised the punchline by the accumulated effect of our changes. The societies which have given us the biblical stories may have been better at the techniques of oral tradition than we are, and thus remembered the stories more faithfully; but they were wondrously free of the modern obsession with historical fact and laboratory detail in comparison to us and had a more liberated view of how meaningful stories should be made more meaningful in the telling.

If we take this aspect of the audience's role in the traditional story and apply it to stories with a presumed historical base, such as the feeding of the multitude in Jn 6, then we can begin to see how radically the literary approach differs from that of some of the historical critics in its evaluations and concerns. The historical critic wants to find out what happened to get behind the account of the gospels to reconstruct the past. The literary enquirer into the same passage wants to discover what the passage is saying to its original narrator and to its intended audience, to get into the narrative as it has been transmitted.

Taking the aforementioned account, the historical critic will note that this incident has multiple attestation (it is told in different forms in different strands of tradition) and will therefore judge it worthy of serious consideration. But then the highly stylised use of numbers will be noted, and their symbolic values taken as an indication that the story comes to us highly embroidered with the theology of the primitive church. The display of power over the sea and the extended discourse about Jesus as the Bread of Life will confirm this suspicion, raising serious questions over any hopes of finding material in this account worthy of an historian's consideration. Coupled with an understandable prejudice against the uncritical acceptance of miracles, different historical critics will produce widely differing reconstructions of the events that lie behind the present narrative; the one thing that most of them are likely to agree on is that things did not happen exactly as reported in the sixth chapter of John.

Literary critics would generally agree with that postulated conclusion of the historical critics, but it would not have the same centrality to their approach. They, too, would note features such as the stylised use of symbolic numbers, the incident on the Sea of Tiberias, and the elaborate explanatory discourse; but instead of taking these as a type of blemish in the account, the literary critic sees in them a highlight of the narrative which shows what the narrative meant to those who recounted it and how its message found relevance to their faith.

The intellectual interest of our age undoubtedly lies more in the findings of the historical critic than in those of the literary critic; historical theories about biblical narratives will occasionally get space in a secular newspaper, but such hope of notoriety is beyond the dreams of the biblical literary critic. We feel that, by getting back to the *ipsissima verba et facta* (deeds and words as actually performed and spoken) we have reached the goal; we can strip away the narrator's concerns and interpretations as so much peeling paint from an old door and work anew at the valuable wood discovered underneath. The fact that we are children of our age determines that this is part of our response.

Yet when we read the Scriptures, we do so not only as children of our age but as children of an ageless faith. And as children of faith we want to discover the meaning of God's message as imprinted in these ancient narratives. It should be possible for us to leap beyond our historical curiosity toward that truth in the narrative which transcends history. In fact, this is happening continuously in the life of believers; to take but one example, it is the rare Christian who listens to the story of the betrayal, trial and death of Jesus during Passion Week without finding rich stores of truth — and very few would trade the sterilised findings of historical research concerning those events for the deep experience of having that narrative pour through one's being with its tale of sorrow and triumph. For those few minutes, we have dropped our historical pomposities and have found ourselves enriched.

The Second Vatican Council's historic document on God's revelation, *Dei Verbum,* clearly identifies religious truth as the object of our biblical explorations. In the case of Biblical narrative, we could describe that religious truth as the message of the narrative striking the heart and mind of the community of faith which receives it. For some narratives (such as the gospel witness to the resurrection), historical truth is a contributing element without which the story has no meaning; but for the vast majority of narratives, whether in the Old or the New Testament, historical concern is either a secondary question or does not enter the arena at all.

Literary criticism of biblical narratives could not survive if it were to be isolated from the findings of other fields of biblical scholarship; yet, in itself, it is a valuable tool in the attempt to discover the truth which God wishes to reveal to his people and the methods which he uses to imbed his message in their hearts. Although the systems of analysis for narrative are many and varied, and even the unanalysed narrative usually fulfils much of its function, the next chapter will present a few rudimentary picks and spades for delving into the mysteries of narrative.

2

ANALYSING A STORY

The Problem of Unity

The great ancestor of literary criticism, the philosopher Aristotle, recorded the observation that every story has a beginning, middle and end. Normally, this is the type of observation which causes few problems; yet in matters of biblical narrative, things are not as straightforward as we might hope.

For one thing, in much of scriptural narrative, there are stories within stories. Again, we look to the parables as an obvious example; these stories had a life independent of their incorporation into the gospel story, and thus there is some validity in treating them as stories in their own right. But can we be cavalier in extracting them completely from the surroundings in which we have inherited them? The same would be true of other stories within stories: the long saga of Joseph in

Genesis, the stories about Elijah and Elisha in Kings, the story of a mother and her seven sons in Second Maccabees.

Source criticism has posed similar problems. We now recognise that earlier literary traditions which once existed independently have been utilised and incorporated by the biblical writings which we now possess. The Yahwist and Elohist accounts — which are largely narrative accounts — in the Pentateuch are well-known examples. Should these, too, be taken as separate literary entities to be analysed apart from their larger context?

The consideration is a primary one, for the end of the story is, to a large extent, what makes it. Imagine the story of Sleeping Beauty ending at the point where the heroine falls under the magic spell; even though everything in the story is exactly the same up to that point, if the story were truncated there, then its whole character would be transformed into a tragedy. What is presented as the complete story entity frames the message; to take in significantly less or significantly more would alter the story's message, conceivably even to the point of reversing it. Imagine again the Sleeping Beauty tale continued long past the wedding: the burdens of high office become too much for Prince Charming. He begins to drink too much. He loses his hair, she loses her teeth; both lose their waistline. She joins Princesses for Peace and pickets his jousts ... The story-experiment no longer resembles that of the original tale which covers all eventualities with its "And they lived happily ever after."

Although one could hardly claim him for the school of the literary approach, St Paul acknowledges the importance of the ending to the story when he states:

> If Christ is not risen, then our proclamation is empty, empty too
> is your faith. We are found out to be lying witnesses for God,
> because we testify about God that he raised Christ which he did
> not do if the dead are not raised. For if dead people are not
> raised, then neither is Christ raised. If Christ is not risen, your
> faith is worthless, and you are still in your sins. Then too, those
> who have fallen asleep in Christ are lost. If we have placed our
> hope in Christ for this life only, we are the most pitiful of people.
> (1 Cor 15:14-19).

What Paul asserts with such strength, the literary critic can
justify with ease: to deny the resurrection of Jesus, or to
reinterpret it radically, means changing the message of the
entire story of Jesus. Yet a careful reading of Paul's statement
shows that many traditional Christians do not interpret the
resurrection in the same way that Paul and the early Church
did: whereas many today see Christ's resurrection as a sign of
his divinity and personal power over death, the early Christians saw his resurrection as the beginning of the general
resurrection of the dead; the end of Christ's story is not just his
glorification, but ours. The de-emphasizing of eschatology in
favour of finding the gospel's relevance to the present age might
well prove to be a very poor exchange; by redetermining the
end of our Christian story, we might be making an eternal tale
a very dated saga.

All of the above demonstrates how Aristotle's observation
bears on story even in the non-literary context. But the question of determining story as a literary entity within the Scriptures has not really been answered. In the study of narrative,
and especially of traditional narrative, a key element is the way
in which the narrative has been communicated to the interpreting audience. In the case of the Scriptures, we have
received our material in intentional literary units which we

generally refer to as "books," which are not haphazard tip-heads of tradition but conscious literary products (even if not always according to our stereotypes of the production of literary works)[1]. For the purposes of this volume, the basic literary unity is assumed to be contained in the biblical book as a whole rather than in any of the separate parts or in any of the prior traditions. Because literary unity is one of the primary considerations in the interpretation of a literary work, the determination of the major parameters of that unity will be an important factor in the interpretation of a particular narrative.

For the purposes of this book, we have chosen five pieces of Old Testament narrative which have been transmitted as literary units in themselves. Yet the problem of the story within a story, or a tradition utilised and incorporated by a later work is still crucial to the problem of the interpretation of biblical narrative. Although there is considerable justification for interpreting such narrative chunks in isolation (an exercise which is done in the case of the short examples given in these first two chapters), the interpretation of a passage as Scripture is not complete until it has been set within the wider context of the literary work in which it has been transmitted.

To be more specific: the question in interpreting a parable is not, surprisingly enough, what did Jesus intend by telling this story on the historical occasion of its first telling. It is a valid question, and an interesting one; but it is not the central one

[1]This statement should be slightly qualified by reminding the reader that some single volume works (such as the books of Samuel or Chronicles) now appear in the Christian Bible as two separate books; that other works which were originally meant to be related without forming a single work (such as Luke-Acts) have this relationship obscurred by the biblical arrangement; and that the principle of literary unity should not really be applied to the hymnals, which would include the Book of Psalms.

when approaching a parable in its gospel context. The real question is what did the evangelist intend by relating the story in the manner in which he did, for this is the only way in which the parable has been accepted and transmitted to us as the Word of God. If we take the example of the parable of the Sower in Mk 4:3-9 and the consequent semi-allegorical interpretation in 4:10-20, this consideration clearly emerges. The interpretation is seen by most commentators as the product of the early church, or even of the evangelist himself, and thus is put to one side by some as being of little worth: the parable must be interpreted again without this later appendage. But literary principles are seriously violated by such an approach; the semi-allegorical interpretation is precisely the key which unlocks the meaning of the parable as part of Mark's message; and it is Mark's message — not hypothetical reconstructions of ancient Palestinian scenes — which has been accepted by the community of faith as the living Word of God. Other considerations may be important, but they are essentially of a secondary importance.

This acceptance of certain works by the community of faith as the Word of God opens the door to a further possibility of literary unity in the story of Scripture: one can, in some sense, see the seventy-three books of the canon as forming a unit together, as one work assembled by the community of faith and the Spirit. This is a consideration which is not totally alien to the nature of the works themselves, as is indicated by their common use of themes and obvious interdependence. Yet the bringing together of the completed biblical literary works is at root a theological and historical phenomenon rather than a literary one; the decision to include or not to include a particular work among the scriptural books was not based on how well it acted as a literary bridge between the work that was immediately previous and the one that came immediately after, but on the grounds that it expressed (or failed to express) the belief of the community which accepted it as Scripture. The Bible does have a unity, but not the type of unity which can serve as a basis of literary analysis; the unity which the Bible possesses is the concern of biblical theology and canonical criticism and lies largely outside of the scope of this book.

Tension, Resolution, and the Sense of Reality

Aristotle's insight into a story's beginning, middle and end is one way of acknowledging that a story moves from one state of affairs to another. In fact, the framework of this movement is the framework upon which everything else (such as symbols and characterisations) is hung. Although there are different ways to describe this movement, the one which we will use is that a story moves from *tension* to *resolution*. This model is chosen because it best demonstrates the implied presence of fear which underlies the meaning of most narratives, as will be discussed later.

The storyteller's first task is to establish the tension. To illustrate the factors at work, we might take a simple narrative from Mark's Gospel (acknowledging that we are doing the pericope some violence by wrenching it out of its literary context):

> Then people were bringing little children to him so that he would touch them, but the disciples told them not to. When Jesus saw it, he got angry and said to them, "Let the little children come to me, don't stop them, for the Kingdom of God

> belongs to the likes of them. Amen I tell you, whoever does not
> receive the Kingdom of God like a little child will certainly not
> get into it. And as he hugged them he blessed them, laying hands
> on them. (Mk 10:13-16)

Here the tension which is established is between the crowd
and the disciples over bringing children to Jesus; although the
tension is represented as being between groups of people
("them"/"the disciples"), it is at heart a tension between
attitudes.

The storyteller creates the tension from elements to be
found in the non-story world, a tension which the story itself
will highlight as being of relevance to the audience. Perhaps
this is a tension of which the audience is already too well
aware; perhaps in the case of the present pericope we catch a
glimpse of a first-century debate concerning the acceptability of
children in the faith community. At other times the tension
represented might be one which the storyteller has perceived
and wishes to communicate to the audience; in such cases the
establishment of the tension itself constitutes a major part of
the function of a particular story. By selecting elements from
the non-story world and juxtapositioning them in such a way
that a narrative tension results, the storyteller has begun the
story-experiment; on the audience's part, the suspension of
disbelief takes place when the hearers accept that such elements could produce such a tension according to their experience or even according to their imagination.

After establishing the essential tension, the storyteller must
allow the elements to interact until the resolution is reached; in
the example chosen, the process is short and swift: Jesus intervenes decisively, explains his intervention, and blesses the
children without further request. This particular tension is

resolved by showing that the disciples had misunderstood the situation; children are acceptable to Jesus, and adults must become children before entering the Kingdom, not the other way 'round.

The resolution can make three different types of statement about the tension which has been established:

1) This is the way things *do* work when this tension occurs;
2) This is the way things *can* work when this tension occurs;
3) This is the way things *should* work when this tension occurs.

In other words, in the first instance, a story is attempting to depict a global truth which will be experienced by anyone who has experienced the tension. In the second instance, the story alerts the audience to a possibility inherent in the tension. In the third instance, the story presents the audience with an ideal which can be realised by those who encounter the stated tension.

The tension which is established may or may not exist outside of the story itself. The all-important suspension of disbelief, however, will only take place if the audience judges that the tension presented represents an analogous tension which has been or could possibly be experienced. Thus the range of stories to which a person gladly listens could conceivably serve as some type of crude barometer for measuring the range of potentialities which she or he perceives in reality; these potentialities might be seen as represented symbolically or realistically in the story. For instance, a parent and child might both be entertained by a film which tells the saga of a giant grasshopper from outer space which devours Detroit; the parent might enjoy it through an acknowledgement that sudden and wide-ranging disaster is a real possibility, even though not in the terms used by the film-maker; the child on the other hand might not have reached the stage of excluding the possibility that giant grasshoppers in outer space have culinary designs upon terrestrial habitations.

The story which is presented and accepted as historical has, as has been stated before, the suspension of disbelief built into it: this tension has existed in the past (and therefore can exist again) and this resolution resulted. But there are ways of avoiding the subjective truth of the historical story without questioning its historicity, as those who deal with biblical narrative know. Basically, the hearer of the historical story affirms that — even though this tension and resolution did occur as presented — there are elements present which make this particular tension and resolution highly improbable in the experience of the hearer. In terms of the biblical story, this might be expressed by stating that some element within the story is unique ("Oh, but he was God!") or that the story universe no longer exists ("Of course, that was two thousand years ago and the world has changed since then"). Both of these represent a failure to suspend disbelief; even though the events of the story themselves seem to be accepted, there is a more central refusal to allow the story to perform its essential function and to present its subjective truth to the hearer.

Working Towards the Resolution

Few stories are so simple as to have one tension and one resolution; even in many relatively short stories, tensions and resolutions are to be discovered as links in a chain or as wheels within wheels. Yet even these are banded together by a great tension and resolution which gives the whole story its unity and its meaning.

Often, the tension of a story focuses the story's movement on a decision to be made by one or more of the characters as a result of the tension. This decision and the events which proceed from it then form the central means by which the tension achieves its resolution. In the Genesis story of Adam and Eve, the choice is quite explicit: the audience has the options clearly identified and knows roughly the results of each. In the following story of Cain and Abel, the choice set before Cain is again made explicit by an intervention of Yahweh after Cain's anger is indicated, but before the murderous deed:

> Yahweh said to Cain, "Why this anger of yours? Why is your face fallen? Isn't it so that if you do good, the face is lifted up? And if you do not do good, sin lies in wait at the door and you are its target. But you can dominate it. (Gen 4:6-7)

Of course, choices can be the centre of a tale without being made explicit by the storyteller. A fine example of this can be seen in the story of the sacrifice of Abraham in Gen 22:1-19. Even though there is little evidence of Abraham's deliberations running through the narrative, even though Abraham is never explicitly offered the choice, his decision and difficulty with the decision is so strongly inplied by the story-experiment that the audience can hardly fail to experience it. The presence of the choice in this particular example is vindicated by the words of the restraining angel:

> "For now I know that you are a fearer of God since you did not hold back your son — your only one — from me." (Gen 22:12)

Decisions do not always take the narrative limelight, but when they do, and when they do their work well, they are a way of allowing the audience to see the results of choices which may face them, or indeed are facing them. This was certainly one of the messages of the Parable of the Vineyard in Mk 12:1-12: the result of killing the Son would be the forfeiting of God's vineyard — be warned! In the safety of the story-world, the decision and its consequences can be put through its paces in near laboratory conditions; the audience sits back and watches the outcome of the experiment and, hopefully, learns something about the effects of such decisions in the non-story world.

These effects are to be seen in the resolution of the tension. The resolution manifests itself in the changes which have been effected by the story's movement, and especially in the changes which have taken place regarding the main characters of the narrative. Such changes might take the form of a new awareness or new attitude in a main character or in the changed circumstances of a main character. While the psychological change (what a character learns through the experience of the story) is more predominant in the introspective fiction of our own age, it is not entirely lacking in the realm of biblical narrative, as the conclusion to Job demonstrates:

> Job answered Yahweh and said:
> "I know that you can do everything,
> and that no plan can be withheld from you.
> Therefore I spoke, but I did not understand,
> wonders beyond me, and I did not know.
> By what ears hear, I had heard of you,
> but now, my eye has seen you.
> Because of this, I am ashamed
> and I comfort myself for being dust and ashes." (Job 42:1-3, 5-6)

Yet even psychological changes are often reinforced by changes in the conditions of the character: the end of the tale will show that the lot of its main characters has been bettered or worsened as a result of their decisions and actions. While betterment takes many forms (a happy marriage, acclamation by the crowds, countless riches, coronation as a monarch, or even an honourable death), the most drastic literary verdict which a narrative can pass on its villains is an ignominious and often violent demise; lesser forms of condemnation would include impoverishment or public humiliation. Again the ending of the Book of Job gives fine examples of narrative vindication and condemnation: the friends of Job are upbraided by Yahweh, while Job himself receives great wealth as a sign of his righteousness (Job 42:7-17).

Nods, Winks and Nudges

While the tension and resolution, together with the movement between them, give every story its structure, the building of the tale upon that framework is heavily nuanced by other factors which can highlight the story's message or even be a vehicle by which the message is introduced. The stereotyped gossip achieves this in an oral account of the adventures of a neighbour by means of nods, glances, intonations, and the savouring of individual words; the written story also has its nods and winks, but oftentimes they are not as obvious to the audience a few centuries removed from the narrative's framing.

In order to be aware of the nuances present in a biblical story's fabric, we must be aware of the mentality which framed the story and the mentality to which it was addressed; we have to identify the reactions which they would cause. When a story sparks off reactions in the modern audience, it is necessary to see if the same reaction would have resulted in the ancient audience; if not, then the reaction, though precipitated by the narrative in its present form, must be disregarded as inappropriate to the narrative as intended. We cannot validly add elements into the story-experiment by intruding into it a reaction which is alien to the original interplay between storyteller and audience. Our purpose is to participate in the original story-experiment as part of the intended audience, not to create a different experiment on our own terms.

Locating the storyteller and audience in their historical world and identifying the lenses through which they viewed that world is one of the prime keys in hearing the nuances of a narrative. Imagine the tale of a Russian dancer who defects to the West during a tour: it makes all of the difference in the world whether this story is framed and told in a setting which embraces the ideology of the East or one which embraces the ideology of the West. In the first setting, the end of the story (". . . and so she slid out the stage door, approached a passing police officer, and immediately asked for asylum.") is calculated to cause horror and condemnation; in the second setting, it would cause relief and delight. Yet, written down, it is the same story and could be phrased in the very same words.

Often, the biblical storyteller shades the narrative by the very words used in the story. Certain key words and jargon terms that would have evoked specific pictures for the original audience may have lost their power for modern hearers — and this is especially true for those who only have access to the story in a translated form. Modern societies, which tend to exchange first names as a matter of course, cannot really appreciate the mystique of the divine name in Ex 3:13-15 in the same way as the storyteller intended; they fail to recognise the very term "name" as a highly evocative word, especially in the context of a divine revelation. Other connotations of "name" are similarly missed in Gen 2:19-20; the giving of a name was a demonstration of Adam's mastery over the other living creatures, not just an exercise in nomenclature. Sometimes the narrative itself establishes certain words and images as pointers to the audience; the element of dreams acts this way in the Joseph story in Genesis, and the word "listen" acts in a similar, though more subtle, way in the latter half of Mark's Gospel.

Character types also act as a clue to the overtones which a storyteller intends. It may mean little to the modern urban dweller that Cain was a "tiller of the ground" and that Abel was a "keeper of sheep," but to the original audience these terms may have conjured up the tension between the herd-tending nomads and settled agriculturalists. There are few hints in this story that "the cowboy and the farmer can be friends!" Biblical figures are often presented as members of an identifiable type — stage characters, if one would have it — such as that we see reflected in Elijah, Micaiah and Elisha from the Books of Kings — the holy prophet who is unafraid of corrupt authorities. Sometimes figures who certainly appear with an identity unique to themselves are portrayed in sections of a narrative with qualities of other great biblical figures: Joshua casts the shadow of Moses when he creates dry land in the bed of the Jordan, or when he makes a solemn covenant between Israel and God; Jesus casts the same shadow when he delivers his law from the mountain in the first great discourse of Matthew's Gospel.

Those elements which give the story its nuances — sometimes its very meaning — can remain completely hidden from the modern audience in the text of a story. This is because the storyteller is depending on elements so deeply rooted in the common consciousness of the original audience that they need not be explicitly mentioned in the tale. One example of this (again, a component of a biblical work rather than the full literary product) is the narrative of the accession of Joash in 2 Kings 11:1-21. The story is related simply and clearly: the queen mother of Judah massacres the royal family after the death of her monarch son; one prince (not of her lineage) is saved and hidden away; he is crowned at the opportune moment and the wicked queen is put to death. A good tale, it hangs together as it stands; but the very factor which gives it meaning, especially in the Books of Kings, is not mentioned at all — the promise to David of an everlasting dynasty, put under threat by the queen mother's actions, but vindicated by God's hidden plan.

Then, too, items which are mentioned to elicit a response from the original hearers have since become encrusted with obscurity and fail to ring bells for us. The clearest examples of this for modern audiences would be the geographical references, all of which tend to translate into twentieth-century ears as suburbs of Jerusalem. The Book of Ruth derives much of its impact from the dramatic decision of its heroine to emigrate from Moab into the land of Judah; but if the difference between Moab and Judah is not perceived by the audience, then neither will the enormity of Ruth's decision be appreciated. One school of interpretation sees the geographical shifts in Mark's Gospel as holding a major key to Mark's message; but if place-names such as Tyre and Sidon and the Decapolis fail to ring significantly different bells than Capernaum and

Bethany, the message will fail to communicate.

Perhaps the strongest of these nuancing elements lie, not in the text of the story itself, but in the beliefs and prejudices of the audience; the skillful storyteller uses the attitudes which he knows to exist in the mind of his hearers, sometimes reinforcing them and using their momentum in the narrative, but sometimes swinging their momentum around until the audience finds itself facing in the opposite direction. This reversal, apparent at the surface level of the story-line, often betrays a deeper attempt to reverse the beliefs and prejudices which are presumed by the storyteller.

Several master storytellers of our own era have made their fame by their skilled use of such reversals, surprise endings, and twists in the tale; O. Henry, Alfred Hitchcock and Agatha Christie are three outstanding examples. Even though entertainment may be a more primary concern of their respective stories, films and novels than the communication of message, these storytellers are opening up new ways of looking at reality for their audiences with methods which Plautus and Terence were using in Rome before the Caesars.

Again, the modern audience must be careful to read biblical stories against the backdrop of the beliefs and prejudices of the original audience, not contaminating the tale with modern attitudes and values. Modern attitudes against violence and warfare — highly laudable in themselves — cannot be imported back into the books of Joshua and Judges. Before the book is even opened, we have too many set ideas about Job's comforters to hear their speeches as reflecting the orthodox religious thought of the storyteller's time; consequently, Job has lost its power to shock us, and the voltage which it once delivered was also the means of communicating its powerful message. Whether or not familiarity breeds contempt, familiarity with a narrative which hinges on a reversal deprives the story of its teeth. How many modern Christian audiences have any sense of surprise in hearing that it was the Samaritan rather than the priest or the Levite who offered help to the fellow who had fallen among thieves? And yet it was that shock which would have sent the original audience away thinking.

When entering into the story-experiments of biblical narratives, it is vital to identify as far as possible with the mind of the original audience and to hear the story through their ears. Unfortunately, for most people who form Scripture's audience today, this requires the work of a go-between, some sort of commentator who will present the world of the story so that the story itself can be heard. Sometimes even the best intentioned readers fail to make the final, crucial step in appreciating the biblical narrative: to move from the intellectual realm of lectures, commentaries and footnotes to experience the magic of the story itself. Information and erudition may exist overwhelmingly in the former, but meaning is to be found only in the latter.

Fear and Function

Humanity is constantly engaged in surrounding itself with a blanket of stories. Even modern, sophisticated society turns much of its technology and resources to the production and dissemination of narrative: the television soap opera, the lavish cinematic production, the foreign correspondent's front page article are all testimonies to our hunger for narrative. And, of course, the less lavish, more ancient story forms are still healthy survivors despite the presence of more modern competitors: people still tell jokes, relate strange incidents, whisper the unapproved antics of neighbours, and recount sports events goal by goal to those who missed the game. As has been observed before, the worth of story is well established by its popularity.

Yet it is not difficult to perceive that some hierarchy exists in the worth of individual stories. We have all seen the film which was highly enjoyable to watch, yet eminently forgettable. But other stories haunt us, creeping uninvited into our consciousness from time to time, forcing us to become the storyteller, perpetuating their own existence. While many stories are content with an ephemeral existence, other stories refuse to die.

Which stories perpetuate themselves most successfully by turning their audiences into their tellers? Oddly enough, we would be mistaken to browse through the great works of literature for the answer. These stories may be the ones most often studied, put on the syllabus for schools and universities, dissected by litterati, and read to the intelligensia at bedtime by cultural radio stations, but are they, in fact, the most often *told*? The successful story, according to that definition, will be found in the oral traditions of a society.

The books of the Bible represent a merger of oral and written traditions: much of the material contained in them once lived the carefree life of the oral narrative before finding a more fixed and permanent existence as the written word. These stories also have great ability in springing back into the oral stream: parents and teachers retell the biblical tales to children, preachers to the adult community. Even the liturgical presentation of these texts is a partial resurrection into oral tradition.

Why are the stories of a society's oral tradition more successful than the polished productions of its literary geniuses? It is not a question of artistry with words or ability with the language; the oral tradition (and canonical tradition for the Christian community) is successful because it enshrines and communicates the values which its mother society has judged to be valid and important. Much of what has been said in this chapter has hinged upon this very role of traditional narrative.

The key psychological element at play in most such stories is that of fear. The human psyche is constantly open to the possibility of peril in existence: we are made alert by strange noises, jump at family members when we have not heard their approach behind us, tremble when opening an unexpected telegram. Even though the vast majority of our anxieties are short-lived and ill-founded, and even though life's joys often outweigh its sorrows, our working days and conscious minds are filled with the problems and small dangers of life. Through the tradition's stories, we are trained in the art of dancing with fearsome possibilities in such a way that we can distinguish between safety and danger; stories guide our steps to ensure that our toes are untrampled and that our feet do not wander over the edge of life's dance floor.

Story's depiction of fear can be obvious or subtle. The disaster novel, the horror tale, the ghost story and the murder mystery all make explicit use of human anxiety. But the romance and the fantasy can also utilise fear, even if this is done in less obvious ways; for the scale of possible perils not only includes the extinction of personal (or communal) existence, but also endangered relationships, social status, approval by authority or any other threat to one's security.

Stories can rarely be reduced to depictions of anxiety; their meaning is richer than such a simplistic approach would allow. But human fear acts in narrative in a manner reminiscent of the workings of electricity; turning on the switch will result in a variety of functions being performed — from lighting a lamp to running a factory — but the same basic principle of ON/OFF is essential to them all.

The fear element of story works on an ON/OFF principle as well: either the fear which underlies the narrative is one to be wary of or one to be overcome. The tensions of the story-experiment establish the fear, or invoke a fear already present in the audience; the resolution of the story demonstrates whether the fear corresponded to a real danger to be avoided or whether the danger was either only apparent or able to be confronted and overcome. In either case, the audience has been vicariously exposed to the danger through the story-experiment and, through the narrative, has measured itself against the strength of the danger; the end result is that the audience has become aware of where the danger lies and learned how to respond when faced with analogous situations.

Fear in narrative does not always work with mathematical regularity, nor can it always be measured in quantitative terms; but this does not reduce the importance of identifying it when interpreting the stories that a community tells and retells. A simple example might be taken, but instead of turning to the Scriptures this time, we will take a tale from the modern folklore of Dublin:

> "A girl on holiday in Spain felt unwell and thought she was suffering from food poisoning. That passed off, so she travelled home again and some weeks later began to feel unwell again. She

visited her doctor and after a number of tests, it was discovered that there was a small lizard growing inside her. It had hatched from an egg which she had eaten in a salad which hadn't been properly washed while she was abroad. She was in danger of death and surgery was not possible. She lived somewhere in Dublin."

That story and various versions of it (in some, the problem is a snail instead of a lizard; in some, the doctor thinks that she's pregnant; in many, the problem is not properly diagnosed until after the girl's death) is a very vigorous one. It has been told between neighbours, schoolmates, a priest is reported to have told it in the course of a retreat, and one version of it even appeared as a report in the newspaper. The version which appears above was taken down from a teacher who first heard it from a lecturer at college. Our inquiry is concerned with the purpose that its persistence serves.

Firstly, the lizard story is hardly told for its entertainment value. It is a clearly unpleasant tale, with an unhappy ending. It also presents a transparent example of a story which utilises fear. The fear at work is the fear of death, avoidable death, which is not overcome by the resolution of the story. Yet the meaning of the story has nothing to do with the great mystery of life and death; this fear gives the meaning of the story its impact and serves as a vehicle for the meaning. In this particular example, the fear of death acts to reinforce a lesser fear which the story establishes in its audience.

The appreciation of the lizard story needs to take into account the society in which it flourishes. Until recently, the typical Dubliner has not been the most adventurous specimen of *homo consumens.* The city's cuisine has been based upon its good quality meat and locally produced vegetables without too much ornamentation of herbs and sauces; Dublin's population has been exceptionally well-nourished, but rarely gastronomically excited. But recent years have seen a change in this situation. Travel to the continent has become far more accessible to the average person and more exotic fare has become available in Dublin's shops and restaurants. Whereas in 1970, a pizza was nearly unheard of in the city, in 1985 many restaurants, both specialist and non-specialist, offer pizzas as part of their normal fare. Dublin's tradition of plain food is currently under fire, and those who refuse to touch anything but the simplest products of cookery are fast becoming the exception rather than the rule.

With this background, it becomes clear that the lizard story is a narrative warning, xenophobic in character, justifying the wariness which many Dubliners traditionally display when faced with exotic food. The narrative establishes that the danger, though not probable, is real and impossible to overcome; even though in knowledgeable medical hands, "surgery was not possible," the peril was destined to triumph.

But fear can be invoked without phobia. The danger can be shown to be real and of enormous proportions, yet the story's final effect can still be one of triumph rather than tragedy. Most of Hollywood's fear-invoking produce is, in fact, affirming human potential: no matter how widespread the damage which results from the peril, there is always at least one person who has conquered it and survived, sometimes saving the whole population through the act of conquest.

There is a good reason for the public's love of a happy ending. While the problem is exposed through the story's tension and development, the happy ending tells the audience that such problems, though presenting real dangers and perils, are capable of being happily resolved. The happy ending affirms the human spirit and demonstrates that humanity can surmount all difficulties and win against overwhelming odds. The sad ending warns the audience to lock the doors and pull the shutters against a particular peril; the happy ending liberates the audience's potential for facing the dangers and troubles of life.

When approaching biblical narrative, we find many tragic endings among the stories within stories: the disobedience of Adam and Eve expels them from Eden; King David's illicit census leads to a voracious plague. The warnings are there, and scriptural narrative — like any other traditional story lore — tries to place flashing lights over the explosives in life's minefield. But it is also interesting to note that the real literary units of Scripture, the books of the Bible, tend to have happy endings, notes of hope to the most tragic of events. The community of faith enshrines warnings in its traditional material, but only within a context of presenting the hidden potential made possible by the relationship between God and his people. Certainly the intelligent reading of biblical narrative must try to perceive how we are warned by the stories within our tradition; yet an even more central concern must be the perception of how we are encouraged and affirmed in utilising the full potential of our faith.

Christians are members of a traditional society which communicates its values and demands through a body of narrative. The literary approach to these narratives succeeds, not by raising questions about the events which are narrated nor by a dissection of a narrative into its component parts, but by allowing the narrative to present its vision in the most effective way possible. Unlike some other approaches to biblical material, a literary approach cannot be content with simply challenging the intellectual resources of those who pursue it; its aim is to enable the story to stir the very spirit.

Summing Up

Twentieth-century Western audiences are at a major disadvantage when approaching biblical narratives. Our philosophical presuppositions demand that a story produce its historical credentials before it is allowed to speak; we impose modern historical methods on traditional narrative and imagine that our questionable reconstruction of events is more meaningful than the value-laden form in which our community has enshrined its vision. In many of the sciences, we are geniuses when compared to the generations gone by; in the area of traditional narrative, however, we have become unappreciative philistines.

The major objective truth which can be discerned in a story — especially in a traditional story — lies in the vision which it communicates to its audience. The effective story is the one that transforms the audience into the storyteller; that transformation is proof that the message of the narrative is in accord with the values of the society which has adopted it as part of its tradition.

Many elements combine to communicate the narrative's message, and the more complex the story line, the more nuanced (and manifold) is the message. But the key to most effective traditional stories lies in the use of fear as it is evoked, verified or conquered through the resolution of the story.

The literary approach to biblical stories tries to allow the stories to communicate their vision as forcefully as possible. By necessity, a literary approach needs the findings of historical and linguistic study and involves analytical methods which can appear to be purely intellectual exercises. The effect, however, is only complete when the modern audience becomes part of the story-experiment, hears the story as it was intended to be heard, and evaluates its vision for itself. Since the worth of story lies in its power to communicate subjective truths, the biblical narrative has not been fully appreciated or interpreted until this subjective judgement has been passed, until the modern Christian audience sees that the story which is being told — although the characters may be ancient and the settings exotic — is still God's story, and still their own.

3

THE BOOK OF RUTH: FAITHFULNESS AGAINST THE ODDS

The human appetite for story is insatiable. No matter how tender the years, it is a universal experience that a good tale will cast its spell over willing ears and eager hearts. One could devote a lifetime to uncovering why the human spirit intuitively recognises and responds to a good story. There is no doubt that part of the answer to this question must lie in the power of the story to speak to the whole person, to imagination, memory and affectivity as well as to reason. Small wonder that children of any age will drop whatever they are doing at the prospect of a story, no matter how familiar.

But what constitutes a good tale? Certain basic ingredients can be discovered in every great story that has withstood the test of time. In our study of Ruth, we will focus on four such ingredients. In the first instance, a successful story is one that enchants, entertains or grips its audience. It must capture and hold the hearer's attention to the end, by means of many skills and ploys, all of which form part of the art of storytelling. We will enter into the story of Ruth at this first level to discover its power of enchantment and its artistry.

A second ingredient which cannot be divorced from the first lies in the meaning of the story. The power of the really great story lies precisely in its resonance with who and what we most truly are. It must speak to the deeper layers of our being, and in the case of the biblical story must focus on a vision of the world which has God at its centre. The story of Ruth invites its audience to reflect on an understanding of life in which certain values, aspirations and choices are explored against a background of deep faith in God's providence.

A third element in our study of Ruth will concern itself with how a successful story, with the passing of time, can undergo some degree of modification or metamorphosis, so that its original meaning receives a new impetus, set now within a wider framework and serving an enriched function. While Ruth is essentially a literary unit from 1:1 to 4:17a, the addition of the genealogy in 4:18-22 and the role of 4:17b in the final contours of the work deserve special comment.

Finally, a great story is essentially great when it continues to transcend the boundaries of space and time, captivating audiences of other cultures and religious beliefs, and shedding some light on the perennial search for meaning within the fragile confines and limitations of human existence.

In our study of Ruth, therefore, we are proposing two layers, the original tale as it runs from 1:1 to 4:17a, and the extended story with its davidic colouring, accomplished by the presence of David's name in 4:17b and the davidic genealogy in 4:18-22. The reasons underlying this twofold approach will be looked at in the third section of this chapter, which will focus on the new dimension which the story receives when set within the davidic framework. The first two sections will be devoted to the first layer, the original story as a literary unit, which can be understood and enjoyed fully within its own terms, without needing either the genealogy in 4:18-22 or the second half of 4:17 for its completion.

Artistry in Ruth

Ruth is a love story of the classical type, which opens on a scene of destitution and loss but ends well. Having elicited the audience's sympathy and attention, the story swiftly moves through the main features of the plot in four vivid acts, to conclude with that joy and fulfilment which a happy marriage and the birth of a son can bring about. How did this literary masterpiece, which must rank as one of the gems of the art of storytelling, succeed in entertaining and holding the original audience? No amount of analysis can ultimately explain why a story works, but some attempt to identify the skills and devices which the author of Ruth so masterfully employed can help to further our appreciation of this enchanting tale.

First of all, the story has a good plot. It is simple and uncomplicated, yet intricately interwoven in such a way that invites the audience to watch out for the cues, and to delight in the recognition of key words or phrases that have a special significance in the unfolding of the narrative. A brief introduction in the first five verses (1:1-5) sets the stage for the first act (1:6-22), achieving a maximum effect through a minimum of words. With swift strokes the artist fills in the historical (when the judges were judging), geographical (Bethlehem of Judah) and sociological (famine necessitates crossing over to Moab) settings (1:1).

We are then given the names of this nuclear family from Bethlehem now settled in Moab (1:2). Disaster rapidly follows disaster. Naomi is first left a widow by the death of Elimelech (1:3), then her two Moabite daughters-in-law share her status (1:4-5). The audience knows that the plight of one widow is bad enough, but to have three so closely linked and with no means of sustenance is unbearable. This initial tension is going to call for some kind of resolution. How can they possibly survive, one a foreigner, and the other two, widows of foreigners? The stage is now set for Act I.

Act One: Return to Bethlehem (1:6-22)

The theme of Act I can be summed up in the verb *return* which occurs no less than twelve times in various forms throughout this section. At first it appears that all three are en route to Judah where there is no longer any famine (1:6-7). The author then builds up a new tension by means of the protracted and tearful dialogue between Naomi and her two daughters-in-law, in which she urges them to return to their own country where they will have better prospects for their futures than if they were to follow her, for she is one against whom "the hand of Yahweh has gone forth" (1:8-13). Naomi describes her sorry lot in such poignant terms that the audience cannot but feel pity for her, mingled with admiration that she should be willing to relinquish her last link with her immediate family, for their sakes.

The tension which has been building up in 1:8-13, in which

there is the real possibility that Naomi may be rendered utterly destitute, will be resolved in the decision which follows. Ruth's magnificent gesture of clinging to her mother-in-law, reinforced through the poetic climax of her pledge of fidelity (1:16-17), brings her firmly into the centre stage, out from behind the shadow of her sister-in-law, who by contrast opts to return to her own people. This first act ends in Bethlehem where the arrival of Naomi and Ruth does not go unnoticed (1:19). The audience is reminded of Naomi's grief yet once again (1:20-21). She may be back home but much has yet to happen before her sorrow is to be turned into joy. The last verse of this act sums up the movement of the story thus far, and prepares for the theme of the next act by stating that it was "the beginning of the barley harvest."

Act Two: Gleaning in the Barley Field (2:1-23)

The author begins by letting the audience into the secret of who Boaz really is (2:1). The main action unfolds in this man's barley field, but Ruth who takes the initiative throughout this scene is not to know his real identity until Naomi tells her at nightfall (2:19). The audience can enjoy the fortunate sequence of events which leads to Ruth's encounter with Boaz and can relish how in her diligence and simplicity she is unsuspectingly making a very favourable impression on him. The movement of the story at this point is carried forward by the first of three well-timed questions (cf. 3:9 and 3:16). In 2:5 Boaz asks about Ruth, "To whom does this young woman belong?" The reply given him by the youth in charge of the reapers describes Ruth in very positive terms and leads into the

first encounter between these two central characters in the
story (2:8-13).

As the day wears on, the audience can take pleasure in
noting how Boaz' solicitude and generosity towards Ruth
increases. Not only may she glean with full freedom and drink
water from his vessels (2:8-9), but at mealtime she is invited to
share parched grain with the reapers and to keep what she has
left over (2:14). Finally, when she resumes work after the meal,
Boaz has already instructed his young workers to facilitate her
in her gleaning (2:15-16). The audience at this stage must
surely ask, "What next, how will this turn out?" The act ends,
as it began, with Naomi and Ruth together, the latter recounting to her mother-in-law the happy outcome of her initiative to
go gleaning (2:3-22). The curtain for this act is drawn by the
final verse which, like 1:22, sums up what has gone before and
prepares the audience for the theme of the next act: the end of
the barley harvest ushers in the work of threshing (2:23).

Act Three: At the Threshing Floor (3:1-18)

Expectations have been very subtly raised in the audience's
awareness. Naomi has obliquely hinted at the possibility of
their widowed situation being resolved through a levirate[1]
marriage (1:11-12). And now through this providential
encounter (2:4-16), in which Boaz demonstrates such good will
towards Ruth whose piety he is swift to acknowledge, is there
not here some ray of hope for the future? At this stage nothing

[1]In a levirate marriage a widow who had no son could be taken to wife by a
brother-in-law, so that the first son born of such a union would inherit the
dead man's name and property (Deut 25:5-10).

is explicitly stated to suggest that this is how the story is going to develop, but attentive listeners will not be totally surprised or disappointed by the turn of events in Act III.

This act falls naturally into three scenes, as was the case in Act II. The central scene at the threshing floor (3:6-15) is prefaced by a preliminary planning session between Naomi and Ruth (3:1-5), and concluded when Ruth reports to Naomi on how things have turned out (3:16-18). In this and the following chapter the author takes for granted the audience's familiarity with the practices of levirate marriage, the redemption of relatives or family property and certain other accompanying symbolic gestures. It is against such a background that Naomi's instructions to Ruth in 3:1-4 must be understood. And it is in this same context that Ruth's subsequent carrying out of these instructions and her initiative in requesting Boaz to act as next of kin must be seen.

At this point, it would be well to alert the modern reader to the fact that this section is not concerned with crafty planning on the part of two females to seduce an unsuspecting Boaz into a sexual liaison with Ruth, so that he will be forced either to marry her, or take her into his family. To suggest that this encounter actually involved some form of prostitution would make nonsense of what has gone before and what will follow concerning the characters of both Ruth and Boaz. Yet there is a risk involved, and the audience is subtly made aware of this in the symbolic gesture of "uncovering the place at his feet." Moreover, the author frequently uses in this section two verbs (*to know* and *to lie down*), which often have unequivocal sexual meanings elsewhere, in such a way that the overall effect of the building suspense in the passage will have the audience reckon with the possibility that Ruth's gesture in approaching Boaz might indeed have misfired. Because this chapter constitutes the climax and turning point of the story, it requires extra attention to discover how the original author intended it to be understood. Ruth is no modern soap opera.

Tension has been building up since the story began. The narrator skilfully creates an atmosphere of suspense. Ruth has been gleaning throughout the barley and wheat harvests, under Boaz' kindly protection. With the end of the harvest in sight, some new initiative is called for. The audience is not told whether Boaz was aware of any responsibility deriving from kinship vis-a-vis the widows. By contrast, Naomi is fully aware (2:20; 3:2) and the audience is also (2:2). So it is up to Naomi to carry the movement forward by suggesting to Ruth to undertake the symbolic gesture described in 3:3-4, to place herself at his feet (literally, "to uncover the place at his feet") when he has settled down for the night at the threshing floor, and await his response.

The suspense mounts as Ruth goes to the threshing floor. In contrast to the other acts of the drama, which unfold against a background of public activity, this one stands out for its air of mystery, secrecy, privacy. The climax is reached in the dim shadows of midnight when Boaz shivers (from cold, since his feet covering has been rolled aside, or from fright when he discovers he is not alone — both possibilities are conveyed by the same verb), and cries out: "Who are you?" (3:9). This second well-timed question leads into Ruth's response and request, and to the point where the story has been leading: "Will you act as next of kin towards me?" The suspense is broken by Boaz' gracious and somewhat emotional reply (3:10-13). The successful resolution of the drama depended on this reply, and the audience can now relax and enjoy what follows.

Even though Boaz can be trusted to be faithful to his promise, there remains a futher element of suspense in the sudden emergence of a "nearer kinsman." A guarantee is given however that one or other will will act as next of kin (3:11-13). Within the dynamics of the story, it would be inappropriate to ask why Naomi did not know of the existence of this nearer relative!

The third act ends neatly with Ruth reporting to Naomi on the success of the encounter, which concluded with a further manifestation of Boaz' by now typical generosity: six measures of barley for Naomi. The curtain falls with Naomi's prophetic statement, which serves to round off Act III and to herald the turn of events in Act IV.

Act Four: Boaz Discharges the Duties of Redeemer and Near Kinsman (4:1-17a)

In this final act of the drama the audience is invited to share in the different ways in which Boaz is as good as his word. First he arranges for a formal settling of who is to act as next of kin for Ruth (4:1-12), and does this with skill and integrity. Here again, as in 3:12-13, it is inappropriate to interrupt the movement of the story by such logical questions as to the identity of this nearer relative, why he did not come forward before this, where did the plot of land come from, and why did Naomi appear to have been ignorant of its existence? The meeting at the city gates ends with the happy decision that Boaz can enter into a levirate marriage with Ruth, with the blessing of all the people and the elders, in true patriarchal style (4:11-12).

This scene gives way to the final climax and happy ending:

Ruth and Boaz are blessed with a son. In this son all the threads of the story are drawn together. More importantly, through him the sustenance of both women in their old age will be assured. Through him Naomi's dead husband will be remembered. In the first act, the women of the neighbourhood witness Naomi's emptiness and sadness of heart (1:20-21). Now in the final scene they are given a last role in uttering a blessing on the child and in giving him a name (4:17a). Barrenness is turned into fruitfulness, destitution gives way to security, and fidelity to the family is rewarded with peace and happiness. The audience can go home now, refreshed by this tale of great artistry and beauty, and reassured that divine providence can bring about a happy ending in spite of what appears at the outset to be a hopeless situation.

Characterisation

Apart from the simplicity of the story and its delicate balance of inter-connecting acts, there are many other features in the Book of Ruth that illustrate how a skilful artist can delight and entertain the human spirit. The author's use of characterisation is one such feature.

It could be argued whether this is a story about Ruth or about Naomi, so cleverly does the author depict the interdependence of the two; yet both women come across as individuals, highly capable of independent action and initiative where this is called for. Naomi is willing to set out for Judah alone if needs be (1:8-15) and on arrival there it is Ruth who proposes to go gleaning wherever is most suitable (2:2). It is Naomi who suggests to Ruth to go to the threshing floor to meet Boaz

(3:1-4), yet it is Ruth who tells Boaz what she wants him to do (3:9).

The Character of Naomi

Naomi is depicted with colour and consistency throughout. Her unenviable plight is hammered home in the opening verses through the repetition of the verb *to be left* (1:3,5); yet she has enough inner resources to face returning to Judah after ten years, alone if necessary should her daughters-in-law follow her advice. The audience must be drawn into some feeling for this valiant widow who is not going to lie down under her sorrow, who can put the well-being of her daughters-in-law before her own, and who is not afraid to admit her grief that "the Almighty has dealt bitterly with me indeed" (1:20, cf. 1:13). The theme of inexplicable calamity and its relationship with divine providence, so central in Job, has its echoes here in the character of Naomi. The audience will want to share in how Naomi copes with her adversity.

Throughout the narration Naomi is in touch with what is happening. At times she is content to sit at home while Ruth moves into the limelight as in chapter two; at other times she intervenes more decisively, as when she suggests how Ruth might put her situation before Boaz (3:1-4), and shows good insight into the outcome (3:18). Finally, the story dramatically ends with Naomi holding the child in her bosom, surrounded by the congratulating women who utter a blessing in joy and thanksgiving that "a son has been born to Naomi" (4:17a). The audience has been reassured that such courage and persistence in the face of adversity does not go unnoticed by Yahweh.

The Character of Ruth

One of the outstanding qualities of the Hebrew short story is its ability to create characters who are both typical and yet highly individual, who are ordinary and insignificant in their occupations and day-to-day existence, yet extraordinary in how they face challenge and adversity. Such a one is Ruth. If the listeners have been moved to pity by Naomi's urgent pleading, in spite of her sister-in-law's decision, Ruth responds to the challenge with tenderness and strength. With poetic eloquence the author portrays Ruth's sacrifice of all that remains to her — her family, her country, her God and even her burial plot (1:16-17) — all for Naomi's sake.

Throughout the narrative Ruth is presented as being so sensitive and caring in relation to her mother-in-law that we might forget that she has also had her own bereavement to cope with. Her choice to be with Naomi is highlighted by the contrast with Orpah. By this clever use of contrast the audience is given to understand that it is not a question of Orpah being selfish or frightened or making a "bad" choice — her option was perfectly legitimate and understandable, and indeed one with which the audience could readily identify. Rather, Orpah serves as a foil to highlight the truly extraordinary in Ruth's decision to surrender all in order to be a support to her mother-in-law.

As the narrative progresses the author fills out Ruth's personality. Her piety towards Naomi with which the audience is already familiar and her quiet industry in the barley field are noted by Boaz (2:11-12) and the overseer (2:6-7). Ruth's response to Boaz' generosity and protection is deferential yet gracious. She is deferential also to Naomi (3:5) and follows her instructions in going to the threshing floor (3:6). Her initiative comes to the fore again in 3:9 for it is she who explains directly to Boaz why she has come. At this point it is important once again to remind a modern audience that what Ruth is asking of Boaz — "Spread the corner of your cloak (literally, wing) over your servant, for you are next of kin (literally, redeemer)" — is in keeping with certain basic principles of Israelite legal traditions. She is asking him to set in motion the legal procedures for a levirate marriage (cf. Deut 25:5-10), even if, within the dynamics of the story, the circumstances in which she makes this request are full of drama and suspense. Ruth's character is further delineated in Boaz' heartful response (3:10) to her candid request. Her moral quality ("a woman of worth") is known to all Boaz' fellow townsmen (3:11). It would have been unthinkable to have attributed anything but the truest of motives to Ruth's symbolic gesture at the threshing floor. From this point onwards the movement of the drama is brought forward by Boaz, as he intervenes judiciously to bring events to a happy conclusion. The author's ability in depicting characters is just as much in evidence in the case of Boaz as in that of the two women.

The Character of Boaz

Boaz has already been introduced to the audience, before he comes on the scene, as a kinsman of the dead Elimelech (2:1). The audience's expectations mount as it turns out that Ruth "*came by chance* to the part of the field which belonged to Boaz" (2:3). At no point in the narrative does Boaz disappoint these expectations. He is discreet; he first enquires as to who this

newcomer is, before he addresses her and makes her feel at ease
in a strange country and in a new and difficult social status of
widowhood (2:5-9). He is sensitive; he respects her need to
work within the social conditions of the time to sustain both
Naomi and herself, but makes it easier for her in many
thoughtful ways. He is considerably older than Ruth. The
author has skilfully portrayed this difference in age through
many helpful cues. As a relative of Elimelech, there is the hint
that Boaz belongs rather to Naomi's generation. He addresses
Ruth as "my daughter" (2:8; 3:11) and is deeply moved that
Ruth should ask for his protection, rather than go "after young
men, be they rich or poor" (3:10). Throughout the scene at the
barley field the author has used the word *young*, whether
referring to male or female, singular or plural, so often (eleven
times), that it provides a strong contrast to the older figure of
Boaz.

When Boaz suddenly discovers he is not alone at midnight
at the threshing floor and is confronted with Ruth's frank
request, he responds with characteristic magnanimity and sensitivity. It is only when he has thanked Ruth for her choice of
him, and has assured her that he will do all that he can for her,
that he then gently raises the question of there being some
complication: "I am, in truth, a near kinsman; but there is yet a
kinsman nearer than I" (3:12). He hastens to reassure her that
he will put the matter before this nearer kinsman immediately
(literally, *in the morning*), and that if this kinsman does not
respond positively to the situation, then he, Boaz, assuredly
will (3:13). He then invites her to "remain on until morning."
The choice of verb used here — to *lodge/pass the night* —
admits of no ambiguity. Nowhere in the Bible does this verb
have sexual implications. Boaz' character is as consistent here as

elsewhere in the tale. Having reassured Ruth of his intentions in her regard, nothing more can be done now until this matter of the nearer kinsman is resolved.

True to his word Boaz takes up this issue in the next act of the drama, and handles it with skill and adroitness. Once again the author uses one character to serve as a reflector for another. The unnamed next of kin contrasts sharply with Boaz. His unwillingness to enter into a commitment vis-a-vis Ruth is understandable. He has a good reason (4:6), but his very reluctance to take a risk over and beyond prudence reminds the audience all the more clearly just how caring and sensitive Boaz has been all through the drama. Ruth's narrator has portrayed three very real characters against a simple day-to-day struggle for survival, yet it is through these very struggles that their greatness emerges.

Stylistic Features

There are many other aspects to the great artistry in the tale of Ruth that could be explored here. Before moving on to look at the deeper meaning and faith values of Ruth, some few outstanding aspects of style deserve brief comment. There are numerous verbal cues by which the storyteller nudges the audience along and entices them to recognise the turning points of the story. The skilful transitions between the main acts have already been mentioned, as well as some examples of repetition and link-words and their effects. Symmetry has its part to play, as in Ruth's poetic declaration of solidarity with Naomi (1:16-17). A more subtle example would be the way in which Ruth's response to Naomi in 3:5 ("All that you say I will do") is taken up and re-echoed by Boaz some verses later ("All that you say, I will do for you," 3:11); and at the end of the threshing floor encounter, when Boaz tells Ruth "You shall not return empty-handed to your mother-in-law" (3:17), there are echoes of Naomi's own lament in 1:20-21, and some hint forward to the deeper way in which Boaz will take away their emptiness.

Symbolism operates at many levels, including that of personal names. Naomi herself explains why she should change her name from *Pleasant* to *Bitter* (1:20). Some scholars see symbolism in the names *Ruth* (meaning either "friendship" or "saturated, abundant in water") and *Orpah* ("the back of the neck = the one who turned her back" or "cloud = not abundant in water"). What first strikes the Hebrew listener about the two sons' names, Mahlon and Chilion, is that they rhyme with each other. The meanings usually attached to their names, *Sickly* and *Pining*, respectively, says a lot about their destiny! Other uses of symbolism will be taken up in the following section which will look at the deeper meaning that the author of Ruth sought to share with a reflective audience.

Deeper Layers: Meaning and Insight

Even at the level of a simple enjoyment of Ruth for its literary beauty and artistic skill, the deeper thrust of the story makes itself felt. In this exploration into the deeper resonances which the narration of Ruth evokes in the hearts and experience of its audience, two questions will be dominant. Firstly, what are the values and vision of life that the author seeks to communicate? Secondly, what is the faith experience of author and audience and what bearing does it have on the attitudes and decisions that shape the story?

Values and Vision of Life

At its simplest, Ruth is a family saga, with the family values of caring, solidarity, loyalty, faithfulness and generosity at its core. The author holds up for reflection what happens in and through the choices and decisions of two very ordinary widows and their extraordinary courage in facing the pain of bereavement, insecurity, poverty and a harsh, uncertain future. The unbounded joy at the end of the story in the birth of a son illustrates a key element in the narrative that might puzzle uninitiated modern ears, namely, the preoccupation that the dead man's name and inheritance be not blotted out. As the story reaches its dramatic end, this theme which has been present from the opening verses in the death of all three husbands, and has been gathering momentum in the actions of the two widows, is now stated explicitly over and over again (4:5, 10, 11, 14).

This aspect to the story reflects an understanding of family solidarity that has its origins in early Israelite clan organisation. The family in the broad sense was the clan, and its members were conscious of the blood ties which united them. The patriarchal narratives are rich in promises and blessings made not just to individuals, but to their posterity for generations to come (cf. Gen 12:2-3; 15:5; 17:2-8; 28:13-14). To perpetuate one's family was understood not simply as a natural duty; it had a religious dimension. It was a means of co-operating in God's plan, as well as providing for the natural protection and security of the family unit. The members of a family in this wider sense had an obligation to protect and defend individual members when in danger. One of the institutions which came into being for this function was that of the *go'el*, (from a verb which means *to buy back* or *to redeem*). The person who acted as *go'el* or redeemer was a near relative, who had a right and duty to protect family interests, whether this involved redeeming persons or patrimony. Although such a person might be expected to act as *go'el* in specific circumstances (cf. Lev 25:25, 47-55; 27:9-33) he could choose to forego his right, as Ruth 4:6 illustrates.

A second institution in biblical times which had a some-what parallel function was the levirate marriage (*levir*, Latin for brother-in-law). Through this practice, which is not very clearly illustrated in the Old Testament (cf. Gen 38, Deut 25:5-10 and Ruth), a brother-in-law in the strict sense of the term, and by extension, a near relative, could marry the deceased man's widow, in order to give her both protection and a son to inherit the dead man's property. Just how strictly (in the sense of brother-in-law only) or how widely the practice was used in biblical times is not known. Only in Ruth do these two quite separate but parallel institutions come together in the dramatic highpoint of the threshing floor scene, when Ruth asks Boaz both to act as *go'el* and to enter into a "levirate" marriage (3:9). From what follows in chapter four, it is clear that Boaz fulfils both functions (4:9-10), and the child who is born to Ruth is hailed as "a restorer of life" to Naomi (4:15).

Family solidarity then is a fundamental value in the story and exerts its influence on the movement of the tale from start to finish. This solidarity which includes a religious dimension is given colour and vigour through a host of related virtues.

Ruth's decision to follow Naomi into an unknown and uncertain future not only demonstrates great courage, it testifies to a sensitive caring for her mother-in-law that will be reinforced and re-echoed as the narrative unfolds, and to a loyalty that goes beyond the call of duty. The fact that Ruth is a foreigner, yet fits so quietly and easily into her country of adoption gives to the narration an atmosphere of unobtrusive tolerance, an element of the story which will be taken up again later. The initiative of both widows has already been pointed out, as well as their self-sacrifice: Naomi in urging both younger women to return to relative security in their own families, and Ruth in opting to stay close by Naomi until death.

Relationships in this story are characterised by generosity, by a largeness of heart that spontaneously goes beyond mere convention or duty. The author's skill in creating two shadow characters to set off by contrast those of Ruth and Boaz has already been mentioned. When compared to their respective foils, both emerge as people who are free enough to move out from behind their own needs for security, and to give without thought of self. Boaz' delicate attentions to Ruth in the barley field are wide enough to include Naomi in their benefits (2:18), and then later on he is concerned that Ruth should not return from the threshing floor to her mother-in-law empty-handed (3:15-17). He is not afraid to jeopardise his own inheritance by taking Ruth into a levirate-type marriage (cf. 4:6).

If family solidarity and loyalty are pivotal points around which the saga unfolds, trust in God's providence is a yet deeper sounding board that the author makes use of to evoke echoes in the hearts of a participating audience. Trust in the face of the grimmest realities characterises Ruth's resolute option to follow Naomi (1:16-17). Lament and sorrow but not despair characterise Naomi's testimony in acknowledging Yahweh's strange ways in giving her such a heavy burden to carry (1:13, 20-21). By engaging in the social options open to her, Ruth is up and doing, eking out a means of subsistence for Naomi and herself (2:2-23), while Naomi is alert to how providence is at work in the encounter between Boaz and Ruth (2:20) and in the follow through at the threshing floor (3:18) and its consequences.

Drawn to the tragic dilemma of the widows at the outset of the narration, the sympathetic listener is gradually nudged into noticing how the attitudes and choices of the main characters of the story reflect their certainty that God is present and active in the events of their ordinary lives, and that ultimately trust and surrender to his mysterious designs will bring its reward (2:12). This pervading sense of God's presence and providence, in a narrative which recounts a series of unfortunate yet mundane events in the lives of very simple, unspectacular people, comes through most effectively in the blessings, greetings and oath formulae which punctuate the story. The blessings in particular have a significant role to play in witnessing to the faith experience which the author seeks to share with the audience.

Theology and Faith-Experience

Although there are only two verses in the narration which have Yahweh as subject of an active intervention in the course of human affairs (1:6, when he visits his people to end the famine and give them food, and 4:13, when he gives Ruth conception), the entire story unfolds in an atmosphere of strong faith in divine providence, even when this providence is very difficult to accept, as in Naomi's lament in 1:20-21. Yet the story is punctuated by six blessing formulae which are eloquent in revealing the extent to which God is experienced as being intimately involved in the unfolding of the human drama.

In the *first* blessing (1:8-9) Naomi invokes the name of Yahweh twice to bestow two distinct favours on the two young widows. She prays firstly that Yahweh may show kindness (*hesed*) to them because of the kindness that they have shown to the dead (i.e. her husband and sons) and to herself. The word *hesed* admits of many nuances, but its basic meaning has to do with a steadfast, reliable, ongoing kindness, tenderness, love, loyalty. It occurs frequently as characterising a certain quality of interpersonal human relationships (cf. Josh 2:12; 2 Sam 10:2; 1 Kings 2:7), but even more frequently it is used to characterise Yahweh's steadfast love and good will towards his people. The Psalms tirelessly celebrate this loving kindness of Yahweh, and it occurs in earlier texts, some of them in a covenantal context (cf. Ex 20:6; 34:6; Deut 5:10; Jer 32:18). Consequently, many commentators see here in Ruth a covenantal background to Naomi's prayer. Although both young widows are foreigners, their practice of *hesed* implicitly makes them true "Israelites," and Naomi can earnestly invoke Yahweh on their behalf, even while sending them back to their people and their gods (1:15). Yahweh is also invoked to reward them by providing new security and new husbands in their own country.

The *second* blessing (2:12) highlights Boaz' recognition of how much Ruth, a foreigner, has done for her mother-in-law since their bereavements. As he prays that Yahweh may richly reward her, he also observes how Ruth has now come to take refuge under Yahweh's wings, a progression in faith from the first blessing when Ruth was still in Moab. She is now living in accordance with her pledge to Naomi when she proclaimed that "Your people shall be my people and your God my God" (1:16).

At the end of that same day when Ruth has returned from the barley field and recounted her good fortune to Naomi, the latter utters a blessing on Boaz (2:20) in which the theme of *hesed* figures once again. This *third* blessing highlights Naomi's sense of divine providence and underscores how she has not lost heart in spite of her sorrow and lament in 1:20-21. It anticipates the *hesed* that Boaz will show at a later point.

Since the *fourth* blessing occurs at the dramatic climax in the narrative at the threshing floor (3:10-11), it is not surprising to find that it highlights a fundamental element in the network of events. Boaz' reply to Ruth's request begins with a plea that Yahweh bless her, since this act of *hesed* on her part is even greater than her first (Boaz is referring to her piety and diligence in caring for Naomi which he has already praised in an earlier blessing, cf. 2:12). This second act of piety *(hesed)* concerning which Boaz is now invoking Yahweh's blessing is the fact that Ruth is seeking to provide a legal descendant for Elimelech, her deceased father-in-law, in choosing to marry Boaz, rather than follow her natural inclinations.

The attentive listener will notice how the theme of this fourth blessing is re-echoed more explicitly in the last two blessings, each of which occurs as the final denouement of the story is reached. In 4:11-12 the elders mark the successful outcome of the negotiations with a blessing for Ruth in true patriarchal style. Yahweh is invoked to grant her fertility in the best Israelite tradition. Rachel and Leah are put forward as models (Gen 35:23-26), and the levirate aspect to the marriage is evoked through reference to Perez, an ancestor of Boaz, whom Tamar bore to Judah (Gen 38). The women utter the last blessing, acknowledging thereby how all the threads of the story have been successfully brought together in Yahweh's providence. He is the one who "has not left you without next of kin this day" (4:14).

Thus, by a subtle interweaving of how *hesed* in human relationships brings the reward of divine *hesed*, the author reinforces a key aspect of the message of Ruth, in and through the sequence of blessings. Through them Yahweh is present and recognised as present in the unfolding of events. His name is also invoked in the traditional oath formulae, by Ruth herself in 1:17 and by Boaz in 3:13. Both occasions are solemn, with both persons making pledges to be faithful to their word. Yahweh's name is also invoked in traditional greeting forms when Boaz meets his reapers (2:4). In the Ruth story God does not intervene in the affairs of his people in very spectacular ways. There are no earthquakes, no visions, no battlefields. Yet his presence is real and experienced in a host of ways, through blessings, greetings and oaths, that reveal how close he is to his people in their very ordinary daily struggles.

The characters in the Book of Ruth are in command of their destinies. They are not passive spectators on the sidelines of life. They do not sit about helplessly hoping that problems will go away. Nor do they rebel and fight against the pain and suffering that have come their way. It is their choices and their decisions, actively made, that move the story along. But those decisions are made in a faith context. At each important juncture, a blessing occurs which reminds the audience that the decisions are made within the context of a strong trust in divine providence. Naomi may complain in very forthright language (1:20-21), but she does so in the spirit of Job 1:21: "Yahweh has given, Yahweh has taken away." Surrender to divine providence, however incomprehensible and harsh this providence may seem, does not take away individual responsibility in decisions. Rather, it ultimately leads to happiness and fulfilment in God's plan. Such is the message of the story of Ruth.

Ruth and the Davidic Connection

Up to this point it has been possible to enter into and to enjoy the story of Ruth, ending at 4:17a, without feeling that anything essential to the original saga was missing. The davidic colouring which the story receives through the presence of David's name in 4:17b and the genealogy of 4:18-22 must now be examined. While this may prove a thorny question, without conclusive evidence as to whether or when the story received this addition, the davidic connection is a feature of the story in its final shape, and as such gives the book an enriched function which merits attention in its own right.

It is easier perhaps to begin with the genealogy. Most commentators recognise that it is some kind of appendix, and that it has close connections with a more detailed genealogy in 1 Chron 2:5-15. A comparison of the two reveals that the Ruth genealogy represents a neat simplification of the Chronicles text or its source, extracting the names of David's immediate ancestors for nine generations back to Perez, and omitting all unnecessary details of uncles, cousins or sisters. This genealogy can hardly be the work of the author of Ruth, since it traces David's ancestry through Boaz and has no mention of either Elimelech or his son, Mahlon, who was Ruth's husband. As already indicated, the whole point of the saga of Ruth centres on the loyalty of Ruth and Boaz, who by entering into a "levirate" marriage, guarantee that Elimelech's name and inheritance will be perpetuated (4:5, 10). Naomi's taking of the child to her bosom (4:16), together with the blessing of the women (4:14-15), further emphasises this point. To introduce a genealogy at the end which bypasses this rehabilitation of the house of Elimelech makes little sense in relation to the story as a whole. The most plausible explanation for it is that it was adapted from an already existing genealogy (either 1 Chron or its source) by a later hand to round off details in relation to David's family-tree.

The more delicate and difficult question is whether it was this same hand which was responsible for 4:17b. As v. 17 reads in the original there is a break in the flow between the two halves of the verse. The first part of the verse reads: "And the women of the neighbourhood gave him a name, saying: 'A son is born to Naomi.'" Then in v. 17b comes a mini-genealogy with the names of Obed, Jesse and David, which possibly represents the point of surgery where the original name of Ruth's first-born was replaced by the davidic line. Once David's name figured in v. 17b, the addition of the adapted genealogy in 4:18-22 was a natural consequence, but not one which matched the original thrust of the saga. Given that the author has demonstrated such skill in weaving all the threads of the story and has dotted the narrative with so many cues and link-words, it is hard to believe that this same author would have refrained so stoically from anticipating in some way the davidic dimension if such had been the original climax and point of the story.

If one accepts the suggestion that the davidic colouring to the story is a later one, some questions must be asked as to how and why such a development was possible. The basic Ruth story has a Bethlehem origin (1:1-2). David too has a Bethlehem origin (1 Sam 16:1). Contacts between Judah and Moab during David's time are illustrated by the fact that David left his parents in Moab under royal protection for a period while he was on the run from Saul (1 Sam 22:3-4). Apart from the Chronicles genealogy and its adaptation at the end of Ruth, nothing is known of the ancestry of David apart from his father's name, Jesse.

It is our suggestion that the Ruth story, which would have been in circulation in Judaean territory independently of traditions related to David's ancestry, was later drawn into the latter as a consequence of the natural desire to fill out the background to this great king. There was already a Moabite connection in a loose sense for David's parents. The mention of Perez in 4:12 in a blessing which evokes memories of another "levirate marriage" could have provided a further impetus to link the two. While it is not impossible that David's ancestry did include a Moabite great-grandmother, it is remarkable that the biblical tradition attesting to this should rest on such slender evidence, and that it should be confined to one half verse (Ruth 4:17b). And indeed, this is a verse which raises problems of its own in relation to the literary unity of a story which does not appear to be first and foremost concerned with preserving historical records. Many psalms reflect this same desire to fill out details relating to David's life, by subtitles which have dubious historical validity (cf. Ps 51, 52, 54, 56, 57, 59).

Whatever the historical accuracy of 4:17b, the Ruth story as we now read it in its final form contains an enriched dimension. All that has been said already about the deeper message and values of the story remains true, but the expanded version contains further reflections. There is a deeper message of universal interest that David's great-grandmother should have been a non-Israelite, that she should have demonstrated such courage, loyalty and filial piety, and that in such non-spectacular ways, God's providence should have been at work in the lives of these very ordinary folk to reward them for steadfastness and upright living by giving them a most illustrious descendant. The infancy narrative of Matthew gives special mention to Ruth when tracing the origins of Jesus the Messiah (Mt 1:5).

Ruth and a Modern Audience

If the test of a good story is that it can turn its audience into narrators, who in turn preserve it for further generations, then Ruth ranks highly in this regard. The wider dimension the original story gains when integrated into the davidic ancestry is one way of illustrating the ongoing dialogue between storyteller and audience. A modern audience can be sensitive to the richness of Ruth when it recognises how much of the core of the story has a permanence and validity that transcends the centuries.

The institutions of *go'el* and levirate marriage belong to the past, but the values of loyalty and solidarity remain. The sociological situation of widowhood may be somewhat more manageable in some of our modern cultures, but the pain and loneliness of bereavement are universal experiences that belong to every age. Ease of travel and communication may reduce the boundaries of today's world, but the decision to leave one's native land and familiar surroundings, and to face an uncertain and unknown future for the well-being of another is an option that continues to challenge the sincerity of our desire to give freely, without counting the cost. Trust in God's providence is easy when things go well, but it is perseverance in adversity that shows how firm and genuine a person's faith really is.

At the heart of this beautiful story lies the quiet conviction that no matter how painful and uncertain the present may be, God's providence is at work. It is in and through the ordinary, humdrum, routine tasks of providing a livelihood and settling matters according to established legal customs that God's will for the individual is worked out. In the story of Ruth there is an attitude of spontaneously turning to Yahweh to bless and thank him as events disclose his providence that could well be encouraged in today's world. It is an attitude not only dominant in the main personages of the story, but shared by the elders and the women of the neighbourhood as well.

The enduring message of Ruth can be summed up in the littleness of the main characters and the stature they achieve through their fidelity and unwavering trust. God is not concerned with national boundaries so much as with the dispositions of the individual. There is an atmosphere of easy tolerance and respect in the story that issues a challenge to racial prejudice in every age and culture. It is, perhaps, a tribute to the author of Ruth that it is so difficult to date the work, and to identify a particular period in Israelite history that would pin down the purpose of the tale against a specific background. This is a story which cannot and will not be pinned down easily, and in that very feature lies one of the secrets of its success.

4

THE BOOK OF ESTHER:
BANQUET TABLES ARE TURNED

From their earliest years people need reassurance, whether it be from fears of the dark or the wooden spoon, or from fears of being abandoned or of getting lost. The intensity of these fears will vary from child to child and from age-group to age-group, but no one, whether child or adult, escapes from this very fundamental and universal human emotion. Adults may devise more subtle ways of trying to cope with fear and anxiety, but they will never succeed in eliminating it from the human condition. The various phobias are but one of the less healthy ways of confronting this unpleasant fact of life.

Another quite different way of coping with fear is to create a story which resembles at some points the fear and anxiety that the author or audience are undergoing. Being able to name the fear has a real therapeutic value, even if the source of the fear still remains; and the value of a successful story is that it can help the audience to identify and face up to what they experience as a threat. The threat may still persist, but some anxiety can be diffused and some relief can be experienced through the narration of a tale in which fears are given flesh and blood, and the internal conflicts can be played out on an objective stage. Such a tale is Esther.

Fear and Reversal in Esther

The plot of the narrative is intricately worked out and fits together very skilfully, but for all its lavishness, and the mystique, elegance and intrigue of the Persian court, its basic story line is very simple. There are two fundamental building blocks around which all the other elements rotate, namely, *fear* and the resolution of the suspense that this creates, through the theme of *reversal*. The author of Esther has an intuitive feel for the inner workings of the human psyche. Only when sufficient suspense and anxiety have been built up, can there be an adequate release of tension to savour the feeling of relief that follows on having escaped from the source of that fear and dread. And such relief is all the sweeter if what was dreaded now falls upon those who were at the root of the fear in the first place.

The fear at the heart of the Book of Esther has to do with facing up to the consequences of being Jewish in a non-Jewish world, and therefore of being different. As the story progresses the audience can identify with the growing threats to the very existence of the Jewish race. Haman's plot to wipe out this "unassimilated people, with different laws" (3:8) takes on magnificent and grotesque proportions by the time it is promulgated by royal edict to every corner of the Persian empire. This threat reaches a climax when it is centred on Esther, their last hope, as she risks her life in approaching the king's inner court, unbidden, to plead for her people (5:1-5).

There is no exact historical counterpart between this world of story and the actual experience of having to live under constant threat, abuse and ridicule, as was the lot of many Jews in the Diaspora. Yet the story of Esther became very popular precisely because through narrative fantasy it was able to identify very deep anxieties and provide a channel for hope and encouragement in the struggle to cope with them. A modern audience, if insensitive to this role of story, can be shocked or repelled by the bloodthirsty element in Esther. The twentieth century has other ways of coping with fear and anxiety. Hindsight and history will judge as to whether some of these are more effective than were those of the time of Esther.

If fear in the face of total annihilation dominates the first half of Esther, the second major building-block, reversal, dominates the latter part. Indeed, it already makes itself felt by subtle cues and suggestions long before the climax is reached. As the narrative winds down to a happy ending, relief is experienced in the many ways in which the fate of the Jews is reversed. The most spectacular of these reversals centres on the fate of Haman, the arch-villain of the plot. The gallows he has had constructed for his bitter enemy, the Jew, Mordecai, are to be used for his own execution, gallows of grandiose and almost impossible dimensions, some seventy-five feet high (cf. 7:9-10, fifty cubits).

As the story ends with rejoicing, festivity and the institution of a feast to commemorate this deliverance, it is not so much a question of the Jews becoming invulnerable and secure thenceforward, though this is hinted at and hoped for in the amount of royal favour with which they are now blessed (cf. 8:1-2, 15,

9:4-5; 10:3). Rather, it is more the sense of relief and relaxation when some impending disaster, which has been steadily increasing in magnitude and terror, is suddenly averted, and what was dreaded now ceases to be a threat.

The theme of reversal has deep roots in the Old Testament, as well as in the human psyche. The primitive urge for revenge, and its restriction to *an eye for an eye*, is not by any means unique to the Hebrews. It rests on the age-old instinct for survival, and is linked with a strict application of the principle of justice. The mystery of innocent suffering preoccupied many Old Testament writers, particularly in the post-exilic period. The classic question, "Why should the innocent suffer and the wicked prosper?", was posed again and again, and one of the ways in which an attempt was made to resolve this paradox was to wish vehemently that the evil plotted by the wicked would rebound and fall upon their own heads. In Esther the theme of reversal carries with it echoes of these earlier struggles to grapple with this frustrating contradiction. A modern audience must be careful not to judge these struggles too strictly against the gospel teaching on revenge. Rather they should appreciate the positive function this theme of reversal plays within the story, a function of encouragement in the midst of hardships, and of hope that fidelity to faith and religious identity will ultimately be rewarded.

At its simplest then, fear and reversal are the key elements around which the story of Esther is built up. The basic plot could be condensed into the following three statements:

(1) The Jews are threatened with extinction.

(2) Through the providential actions of Esther and Mordecai, both steadfastly loyal to their religious tradition, the Jews are not only saved, but the fate plotted

> against them recoils upon their enemies.
>
> (3) They celebrate their deliverance with rejoicing and a festival, which in time becomes institutionalised into the Feast of Purim.

But such a prosaic summary does not do justice to the inventiveness of the storyteller or to the enjoyment value of the story. There is no better way of appreciating the saga of Esther than to read it or hear it told from beginning to end, and thereby to allow the creativity of its author to captivate the imagination and stir the emotions.

The paragraphs which follow will be concerned with investigating some of the strategies and devices the narrator has used to hold and stimulate the original audience. We will be concerned first and foremost with the story as it has come down to us in the Hebrew tradition. The Greek additions, which belong to a later stage in the evolution of this popular tale, will be left aside for the present. Their contribution will be examined separately, once the main thrust of the story has been explored.

The movement in the story of Esther is carried forward through three main acts, which correspond in content with the three statements outlined above. But first a prologue sets the stage, introducing the audience to the grandeur and pomp of the Persian court, and to the precarious nature of what it means to enjoy royal favour.

Prologue: Esther Becomes Queen (1:1-2:23)

The main function of the prologue is to introduce the heroine of the story to the audience and to let them in on what is one of the key secrets of the main plot, long before the

Persian king and court become aware of it. Esther's real identity is not to be disclosed until the climax of the story, at which
point the dramatic revelation of her being part of the Jewish
race is calculated to galvanise the king into action. Meanwhile,
she is under strict orders from her uncle, Mordecai, not to
reveal "her people or family" (2:10, 20). But Esther is not
introduced immediately. There is an intentional build-up to
her entry and rise to royal status, in the form of two contrasting scenes, and two contrasting queens. Queen Vashti's downfall is Esther's opportunity. Already the theme of reversal is
being subtly introduced. But how does Queen Vashti's downfall occur?

The tale opens with a royal banquet of gigantic proportions.
The first eight verses depict a setting of luxury, splendour and
utter prodigality. It is hard to visualise how a kingdom could
function if all its chief dignitaries, including king and army, not
to mention its entire administrative staff, can spend "a hundred
and eighty days" (1:4) in unbridled feasting! And then afford a
second rather low-key banquet for all the citizens of the capital
for a further seven days (1:5). When we add to this a third
banquet in Queen Vashti's quarters for all the women in the
royal palace (1:9), it is small wonder that tempers are getting
shorter and nerves frayed. It is not surprising then that a huge
storm blows up when the king's whim to have his queen
displayed before his revelling court is thwarted by Vashti's
non-appearance.

There is humour in this contrast between pomposity and its
failure, between an elaborately administered empire and a
minor domestic conflict. Both king and court are in a flurry.
The queen's refusal takes on world-wide proportions, and not
only leads to her own downfall, but to the solemn drawing up

of an irrevocable royal edict, to be promulgated in every corner of the vast empire, in all the different scripts and languages (1:19-22). There is more than just humour in the contrast between the administrative machinery set in motion to have the decree promulgated, and its actual contents. The narrator moves into satire when this domestic disagreement is presented as capable of toppling the vast realm of the Medes and the Persians. Just imagine! "King Ahasuerus gave orders for Queen Vashti to be brought before him and she did not come!" (1:17). And what great improvement to the empire is this decree intended to accomplish? An important one within the story, but not something likely to commend itself to modern sensibilities: "That every man be master in his own house" (1:22)!

Queen Vashti's replacement does not take place immediately. The storyteller prepares for Esther's entry with suitable build-up. First of all, beautiful girls have to be sought (2:2). Then they have to undergo a twelve-month course of beauty treatment (2:12), and if they are pleasing to the king on their first appearance, they may be summoned by name to come before him again (2:13-14). There is a fitting climax to this elaborate choice of a new queen when Esther finally comes before the king. Only she wins his unqualified approval and is proclaimed "Queen instead of Vashti" (2:17). These opening scenes draw to a close with yet another royal banquet, this time in Esther's honour, and like the other banquets, it is marked by the same spirit of largesse (2:18).

Before moving into the plot of the story proper, the narrator is thus carefully preparing the stage. A note of anticipation and suspense has been struck in the careful concealing of Esther's identity (2:10, 20). Although Esther has moved into centre stage as being unquestionably the most beautiful girl in this vast empire, there is another person with whom the audience must begin to reckon. At first Mordecai is simply Esther's "uncle," an insignificant Jewish exile, whose ancestors had been deported from Jerusalem in earlier times (2:5-7). As the narrative progresses however, it becomes clear that he is her stage-manager, keeping a close eye on the turn of events from a discreet distance (2:11, 19). And he is not without initiative. By alerting King Ahasuerus through Esther, he successfully foils an assassination plot directed against the king (2:21-23). A record of his quick action is duly made in the king's presence and apparently forgotten. However, this act of loyalty will receive its due reward at a more crucial point in the story. The stage is now set for the main plot, with only one more significant character to be introduced to the audience.

Act One: Haman's Plot against the Jews (3:1-4:17)

The chief villain of the story now enters. His name is Haman from the land of Agag, a country otherwise unknown. He is singled out for exceptional honour and rank by the king, without any apparent reason (3:1). When this partiality reaches the point where all those employed in the king's service at the city gates must, by royal command, prostrate themselves before Haman, Mordecai refuses (3:2). There are echoes here of an earlier refusal and the disproportionate reaction it provoked (Vashti's non-appearance and subsequent banishment). Haman is infuriated by the stand taken by Mordecai, and resolves on an act of revenge as grandiose as his own ambitions for power. He makes up his mind to destroy not just Mordecai, but the entire Jewish population of the empire (3:6).

There are some interesting contrasts in these first six verses of chapter three. Mordecai does not have to give reasons for his refusal to prostrate himself before Haman. Nevertheless the storyteller has created a very subtle contrast between the pomposity and hollowness of Haman and Mordecai's level-headed loyalty (cf. 2:21-23). By identifying with the courage of Mordecai, perhaps the audience is being invited to look beneath the allure of high places. Noteworthy too is the contrast between Mordecai's open avowal of his Jewish origins and his command to his niece to do just the opposite. On no account is she to disclose that she is Jewish. This anomaly will be resolved later.

Even at this early stage, there is nothing particularly likeable about Haman. He does not appear to have done anything constructive to merit his meteoric rise to prestige, but once he has had a taste of being at the top, he cannot countenance any gesture that would suggest otherwise. The narrator shows great psychological skill in the depiction of this narcissistic character, who must be at the centre of attention at all costs in order to survive, and who flies into a rage when even one person refuses to give him the required supplies of adulation (3:5). It is precisely these narcissistic ambitions which will ultimately bring about a total reversal of Haman's situation.

The second phase of Act One (3:7-15) is concerned with how Haman sets about getting his own way. Nothing less than a decree of extermination against the Jews will satisfy him. His approach to King Ahasuerus is a little more "logical" than his fury against Mordecai. He presents his case to the king that "this unassimilated nation," which is different and ignores royal edicts, is a threat to the other nations of his realm (3:8). He would have been more honest if he had confined his prejudice specifically to just one person, Mordecai, whom he perceives as a personal threat to his own prestige.

The king consents, and waves aside Haman's bribe of ten thousand talents of silver. And so the fearful plot is set in motion with the king's seal and the promulgation of the decree (3:10-15). The mention of *runners* to dispatch it (3:13, 15) quickens the pace of the narrative, and adds to the sense of alarm as the inevitable draws nearer. Words like *slaughter, destruction* and *annihilation* are not spared, and all are to fall under the terrible ban on the day of doom. The actual day on which the annihilation was to be carried out had been decided by lot already, by Haman (3:7-8). The *pur* or lot had fallen on the twelfth month (the link between this Akkadian or Babylonian loan-word and the feast of Purim will be looked at later). This was not to be the only occasion that Haman made advance arrangements to suit his own schemes, before getting the king's permission, arrangements which then backfired against him. An attentive audience will come to recognise this theme of reversal as dominating Haman's life. The scene ends with a grim contrast: yet more banqueting and revelry in the royal palace, while panic and consternation grip the hearts of those who are doomed (3:15).

The last phase of Act One shows the audience how Mordecai and Esther take steps to try to avert the impending annihilation (4:17). Mordecai's reaction is typical: a public demonstration of mourning according to Jewish tradition (sackcloth, ashes and weeping), which is re-echoed by the Jewish community throughout the empire (4:1-3). Esther's response is more discreet and in keeping with her concealed identity. A

eunuch, Hathach, serves as a go-between in the anxious deliberations between Mordecai and Esther (4:5-17). The narrator
keeps the audience in suspense as Hathach goes to and fro,
from one to the other, reporting both sides of the dilemma.
This go-between delays the action but thereby heightens the
suspense. Mordecai begs Esther to plead with the king, but
Esther knows the penalty to be paid for approaching the king
unbidden. Eventually she is challenged into some kind of
action by Mordecai's final message (4:12-14). But the audience
is left in suspense as to what kind of action she will take and
whether it will be effective.

The juxtaposition of these two characters in this dialogue
deserves comment. Both are strong and both are under duress.
Yet neither dominates the other. Even if Esther finally decides
to risk approaching the king, under Mordecai's insistent pleading, it will be up to her alone to devise the most effective
strategy to persuade the king to grant her request. Mordecai,
for his part, trusts in providence. Even if Esther were to fail by
refusing to approach the king, deliverance will come "from
another place" (4:14). This is the closest that the narrator of
Esther comes to mentioning God's providential care for his
people. Mordecai's final sentence reinforces this theme of God's
providence: "Who can say but that it was for just a time such
as this that you have come to the throne" (4:14). Thus, at this
moment of dramatic suspense the storyteller delicately directs
the audience's attention to this providential aspect in the action
that Esther is about to undertake.

Act Two: *The Reversal of Haman's Plot* (5:1-8:2)

This is the central and crucial part of the narrative. It is punctuated by two banquets and two falls, each one subtly interconnected with and dependent upon the other. After Esther's first banquet (5:1-14), there follows Haman's initial fall (6:1-13). Then as Esther's second banquet (6:14-7:7) brings the story to its climax, it is sealed by Haman's final fall (7:8-8:2). Just as there is progression and excitement in the movement from one banquet to the next, so too, Haman's initial discomfiture is but the harbinger of his final downfall. The twin themes of fear and reversal intertwine neatly in Act Two, forming a crescendo as the denouement of the plot draws near.

Esther's First Banquet (5:1-14)

Anxiety and dread reach their most intense moment as Esther now prepares to risk her life in approaching the king's presence unsummoned. Everything is staked on that risk. Will the three day vigil and fast inside and outside the palace have been of any avail? As soon as the king sees Esther before him however, "she found favour in his eyes" (5:2). It is from this point onwards, as the king "held out the golden sceptre that was in his hand" (5:2), that the audience can begin to breathe a little more comfortably. Once it is clear that Esther's act of disobedience, unlike that of her predecessor, Vashti, will not be punished, tension begins to slacken a little. But will Esther succeed in her venture? In response to the king's invitation,

Esther makes her request. It is deceptive in its simplicity and modesty! Just a banquet for the king and Haman.

Haman, true to character, is overjoyed to receive such prestigious attention. He is even more elated to learn that this honour is to be repeated, by an invitation to a second banquet. How could he have been aware that this was merely part of Esther's strategy, and that her real request at this second banquet in fact will lead to his downfall? The narrator's talent in character portrayal is at its best in the scenes which follow. Haman, excited like a spoiled child, rushes home to broadcast news of the honours he has just received. En route, a dark cloud crosses his sunny path, and momentarily causes an onrush of anger. That Jew, Mordecai, was still refusing to bow before him! At home, his wife and friends are subjected to a full recital of all his successes, crowned by the most recent one, namely, these two intimate banquets with just Esther and her king (5:9-12).

Here is narcissism at its finest. Haman, basking in self-worship, and nourished by the flattery and adulation of his supporters, cannot tolerate someone who refuses to do homage before him. His inflated self-image cannot withstand such a threat. And so, unable to await Mordecai's death with all his fellow Jews on the decreed day of destruction, he impulsively acts on his friends' advice to have gallows erected, and then asks the king to have Mordecai hanged on them next morning (5:13-14). With that fly in the ointment suitably disposed of, Haman should be able to go to the banquet without a care in the world. Or so it would seem.

Haman's Initial Fall (6:1-13)

The sequence of events from this point onwards is shot through with the theme of reversal. Fortunately for Mordecai, the king was unable to sleep that night and to soothe him, he had the *Record Book* read aloud to him (6:1), in which Mordecai's act of loyalty (2:21-23) was recounted. As the king sets about making amends for this unrewarded action, the one he first encounters next morning is Haman, who for his part is intent on having just the opposite fate arranged for Mordecai as soon as possible. The lofty gallows are already erected. All that is needed is the king's approval for the execution.

The narrator's timing is splendidly worked out. When the king asks Haman's opinion as to "how a man should be treated whom the king wishes to honour" (6:6), he answers as only a full-blooded narcissist could, with total self-reference. For the moment, Haman forgets his own agenda, and allows his fantasy full rein: "Royal robes and royal horse . . . and the noblest of the king's officers to decorate him . . ." (6:8-9). It would be hard to imagine a greater blow to Haman's self-esteem, when the king curtly tells him, "Hurry. . . do everything you have just said to Mordecai, the Jew" (6:10). Small wonder that Haman hurried home dejected and downcast after having had to bestow on his bitterest enemy the trappings of his own grandiose wishes for acclaim and recognition. This total reversal of roles is correctly interpreted to him by his wife and friends:

> 'If Mordecai, before whom you have just had an initial fall, is of the Jewish race, you will not prevail against him, but you will assuredly fall before him again' (6:13).

This shrewd and rather pessimistic observation can hardly have helped to put him in festive mood for the second banquet!

Esther's Second Banquet (6:14-7:7)

Before Haman has had an opportunity to absorb the full impact of the ominous interpretation of his wife and friends, he is swept off to Esther's second banquet. This resembles the previous day's banquet up to the point where Esther responds to the king's enquiry as to what she would like. Both Esther and the audience are encouraged by the success of the strategy thus far, and particularly by the royal recognition of Mordecai's loyalty which has occurred at a most unexpected but timely moment. Esther is now more certain of the king's good will, and comes into the open with her real request and her real identity.

Her pleading is eloquent. She presents her impending death as a loss which the king will sustain personally (7:4). She does not name her adversary immediately to allow time for the king's wrath to reach adequate proportions. Then comes the key denouement as the king demands the persecutor's identity, and Esther replies: "An adversary and enemy, this evil one, Haman" (7:6). Emotions are running high. Haman is trembling with fear, while the king is trembling with rage and rushes from the banquet hall. Only Esther appears to be calm, for her anxious moments of suspense have turned out well. The author then adds one last dramatic touch to round off this total reversal of Haman's plot.

Haman's Final Fall (7:8-8:2)

Esther's second banquet is abruptly terminated with the king's hasty exit into the royal garden. His equally abrupt return is so timed as to have him think that Haman's desperate pleading for mercy at Esther's couch is nothing but a brazen attempt to rape her (7:8). What a reversal indeed! The fate of him who sought to have the entire Jewish population exterminated is now well and truly sealed. In a succession of evocative images the audience is confronted with various levels of reversal. The tables are turned for the one who could order the destruction of so many so easily; for now he must grovel on his knees to beg for his own life before one of those he thought to have executed. Moreover, what Haman sought for his enemy Mordecai is now to befall him quite literally. The imposing seventy-five feet high gallows which he had had erected for Mordecai are now to serve for his own speedy execution. And finally the king completes the reversal when he hands over Haman's house and possessions to Esther, and bestows his signet ring, which he had recovered from Haman, on Mordecai (8:1-2).

Act Three: The Jews Enjoy Royal Favour (8:3-10:3)

Once the central tension of the tale has been successfully faced and resolved, the remaining scenes depict the sense of relief which naturally follows. This relief finds expression particularly in the description of rejoicing and feasting that takes place throughout the empire. But first, the annihilation decree must be publicly revoked. Esther again faces the king, pleading with him to have a written revocation of Haman's wicked scheme drawn up and given royal approval. Only then can her race feel safe.

With typical solemnity a new edict is divised and dispatched throughout the empire. And from this point in the story onwards the audience should note how Mordecai gradually moves into the centre stage. Once Esther has obtained the revocation of Haman's decree it is really her uncle who takes over. Whereas Haman's initial decree was sent out by mere "runners" (3:13), this new communique is to be dispatched by no less than "couriers mounted on swift horses," bred from the king's own stud farms (8:10). Mordecai's influence in high places is subtly shown to be more effective than ever Haman's was. Whereas the initial decree was directed against the Jews, this new decree emanates from them, in the person of Mordecai. By means of it, they are granted the right to disarm their enemies, with effect from the very day originally decreed for their annihilation, "the thirteenth day of the twelfth month, which is Adar" (8:12). The theme of reversal has not yet been exhausted.

Instead of fear and panic before the impending slaughter, there now reigns "light and joy, rejoicing and honour" (8:16). Joy is the keynote of the celebrations throughout the community, as news of the edict reaches the extremities of the vast empire. Banqueting, a familiar feature in Esther, is no longer the exclusive prerogative and privilege of the royal palace. From now onwards, it will characterise the Jews' celebration of release from fear and oppression (8:17, cf. 9:17, 18, 19, 22).

As the day of fate draws near, the final note of reversal is sounded loud and clear:

> The day on which the enemies of the Jews had plotted to crush them was turned upside down; for it was the Jews themselves who crushed their enemies (9:1).

The tables are completely turned. Far from cringing in fear and dread, the Jews are now the ones before whom others tremble (9:2). Even the king's officials and governors are afraid of Mordecai, whose fame is becoming a by-word in the provinces.

The description of the massacres follows the same imaginative pattern as the initial decree for the extermination of the Jews. The slaughter of five hundred in the capital is climaxed by the special mention of Haman's ten sons who undergo a "double execution," by the sword on the thirteenth day, and on the gallows the following day. This second day's execution is accompanied by a further slaughter of three hundred in the capital. The storyteller thus protracts the flavour of reversal by having the king grant Esther this extra day of reprisal in the capital. When added to the number of those killed in the provinces, the total reaches the staggering figure of seventy-five thousand, eight hundred and ten! The audience can take vicarious satisfaction in such a successful outcome to the overthrowing of Haman's plot.

A modern audience will find it difficult to identify with such bloodshed and with the obvious rejoicing that follows in its wake. This is particularly true in the case of an audience that knows from bitter experience the pain and heartbreak that contemporary forms of violence and terrorism leave in their wake. Once again, it is necessary to remind such an audience of the inner dynamics of the story and of the need for suspension of disbelief if one is to enter into the story-experiment on its own terms. There is much exaggeration in the narration of the events around which the saga is built. The situations are extravagant, the two poles of the tension are oversimplified. But it is precisely an important function of this story to depict elements of that tension in such a way that an original audience could be helped to clarify their own stance in relation to the ambiguities and conflicts that resulted from their being "different and unassimilated" in their environment, as a consequence of their religious beliefs. The strong positive note on which the story ends is intended to encourage the listeners. No matter how threatened they may feel themselves to be, this tale has a message of hope for them. To those who trust in divine providence (cf. 4:14), deliverance will surely come. Resolute action that respects their religious convictions will bring its reward.

The Feast of Purim

It is possible that the first drafts of the Hebrew tale of Esther ended at 9:19. For all practical purposes the basic story line is complete by this point, with a celebration of thanksgiving firmly established on the 14th/15th of Adar (9:17-19). The remaining paragraphs are explicitly concerned with the official institution of Purim, and bear traces of being secondary. The elements of feasting and rejoicing already highlighted in the preceding sections (9:16-17) are now taken up again and fleshed out into what was to become a very popular annual celebration of the feast of Purim. Its name is derived from a loan-word used early on in the main narrative, *pur* or lot (3:7), and evokes a very significant element in the tale as a whole, namely the fear and insecurity that derive from a capricious unleashing of prejudice and hatred.

It is very difficult however to establish the exact relationship between the origins of this feast and the tale itself. Many scholars consider the feast to be an adaptation of a non-Jewish festival, borrowed by the Jews of the Eastern Diaspora from their Babylonian and Persian environment. It is worth noting that the feast of Purim does not figure in the Qumran liturgical calendar. The extent to which Purim is actually linked to an historical deliverance from persecution remains an open question. The story can stand without the official feast. And the non-religious, non-cultic aspect to the feast, together with the foreign element in its name, suggests that the feast could have been borrowed without reference to the events in the story. Indeed a number of scholars consider that the reference to *pur* in 3:7 is a later insertion. As the narrative now ends, however, both feast and story are inextricably linked. And that linking of feast and story is strong testimony to the popularity of the Esther tale within certain circles, and to an ongoing dialogue between storyteller and audience. Esther was the kind of story that provoked further elaboration. The best illustration of this process lies in the considerably expanded form of the Greek text of Esther. These expansions, usually known as the Greek Additions to Esther, deserve some comment, both in their own right, and for what they contribute to the story as a whole.

The Greek Additions to Esther

In all there are six extended passages (reaching a total of 107 verses) which have no counterpart in the Hebrew story. Their most striking overall contribution to the narrative is to inject into it a pronounced religious dimension. All but one explicitly mention God's name and his power over human affairs, and in the case of this one omission (the so-called text of Haman's decree), it is understandable that God's name does not figure. This is in strong contrast to the Hebrew tale of Esther, which never mentions God's name explicitly, and which focuses more directly on the human characters as governing the course of events by their own decisions and actions.

This preoccupation to give Esther a more religious context is not confined to the Additions only. The Greek translation, which has come down to us in two divergent textual forms, inserts God's name at various other points as well. In 2:20, for example, when Esther does not reveal her ethnic origin in obedience to Mordecai's orders, the Greek text adds that the latter had bidden her "to fear *God* and obey his commands." And again in 4:8, the Greek translation has Mordecai urge Esther "to invoke *the Lord*" before approaching the king. When the king is unable to sleep in 6:1, according to the Greek text "it was *the Lord* who drove sleep from the king that night." These are only a few illustrations of this tendency in the Greek translation.

The secondary nature of the Additions is beyond doubt. They are usually dated some two hundred years later (i.e., about the second/first century B.C.). Since they vary from one another in purpose, content and style, it becomes clear that they cannot have all come from the same hand, and do not reflect a homogeneous reworking of the basic story.

Additions A and F[1] are loosely linked in that the former relates Mordecai's dream which foreshadows the main events of the story, while the latter, at the end, provides a detailed explanation of this dream. The dream imagery and the apocalyptic flavour of the passages are not unlike other second century visions, notably those recounted in Daniel. Particularly noteworthy is the change of emphasis, whereby the struggle is no longer just between the Persians and the exiled Jews, but on a cosmic scale, between "every nation" and "the nation of the just." Both additions highlight that it is God who is in control of all such events, and that he saves his people when they cry to him in their distress.

Additions B and E are presented as the actual texts of the two royal edicts, dictated by Haman and Mordecai respectively. Unlike the other four additions, they bear no traces of having had a Semitic original, and are marked by a literary polish and rhetoric noticeably absent from the others. Various reasons can be suggested for their inclusion, but the simplest might be that they represent a natural desire to expand on a successful story and to supply the audience with important details not recounted in an earlier telling. It would have mattered little to either narrator or audience that these might be fictional texts. They lent an air of credibility and solemnity to the story and thereby increased its entertainment value.

As already mentioned, Addition B does not bring in an explicitly religious dimension. But it is a clever piece of propaganda, in keeping with the basic elements of the original story,

[1]The Greek Additions are usually designated by chapter letters (A to F) rather than by chapter numbers.

inasmuch as it retains the scapegoat theme. These people are different and difficult, a threat to the empire, so wipe them out!

Since Addition E is "dictated by Mordecai," it can afford to express some religious reflections, even though the main focus is on a withering attack against Haman! Once again, the key-note of God's providential guidance is expressed in varying ways (E 4, 16, 18), culminating in the joy of deliverance, "for the all-powerful God had made this day a day of joy and not of ruin for his chosen people" (E 21).

The third Addition (C), which contains the Prayers of Mordecai and Esther, represents the most spiritual input of the Additions, and gives witness to the best of Jewish piety at the time of its composition. In both prayers there is a sense of urgency and pleading, appropriate to the crisis, and a deep trust that God will be faithful now as he has been in the past. Many typical biblical themes are interwoven in these verses, themes strikingly absent from the Hebrew tale. Mordecai pleads with God the omnipotent creator (C 2-4), the God of Abraham (C 8) and the God who made Israel his ancient heritage (C 8-10).

Esther re-echoes these prayers (cf C 16, 23, 29) and adds the themes of repentance for sin (C 17), Temple (C 20), and observance of Jewish laws regarding marriage, ritual cleanliness and diet (C 26-28). In stark contrast to the Hebrew tale, these prayers overflow with the name of God. The more intimate form, *Lord*, occurs no less than ten times in Mordecai's prayer and seven times in Esther's. Her pleadings are particularly poignant as she expresses her fears of being alone (C 14 and 25), isolated from her people and about to risk her life for them. In the evolution of the Esther saga, these prayers repre-sent a very special way in which a successful story could draw forth and give shape to a living spirituality. The story teller and audience who could compose prayers such as these as a response to the basic narrative were surely able to enter into the movement of the story and find some echo of its dilemmas in their own experience.

The fourth Addition, (D), is a superb dramatisation of Esther's entry into the king's presence. It surely qualifies as one of the climaxes of the Greek narrative as a whole, and beside it the Hebrew text of 5:1-2 becomes dull and prosaic. First, there is the careful transition from prayer and mourning apparel to festive robing (D 1). Esther then approaches the royal presence suitably attended by her two ladies-in-waiting. Her dazzling beauty is extolled twice over, and though outwardly radiant and serene, her heart is pounding with fear (D 2-5). The numerous doors that she has to pass through draw out the suspense, which reaches a high-point when she finally enters before the king who is "blazing in anger" (D 7). At this most crucial moment, just as Esther faints with terror, the principal character in the Greek text takes over: "But *God* changed the king's heart to gentleness" (D 8). From this point onwards, all works out well. The king takers her in his arms, and he and his court gently try to reassure her (D 8-15). By comparison with the original story the emphasis in the Greek text changes from Esther's courage to God's providence. The hero of this scene is neither Esther nor the king, but God.

This brief examination of the Greek Additions illustrates very effectively how the original emphasis of a story can be appreciably altered when an audience is changed into story-tellers. The tale of Esther becomes a "two-in-one" when the richness of the Greek Additions is accepted as part of the ongoing development of the narrative, and as representing the contribution an extended audience can make to the shaping of

a story. The biggest contrast between the two versions undoubt
edly lies in the religious dimension. The Greek tradition overflows with a rich biblical spirituality. There is a strong faith in
God's providence that, no matter how great the cosmic struggle, those who are faithful to the end will conquer. God will
remember his people and vindicate his heritage (cf. F 9). When
one returns to the world of the original Hebrew story one
cannot but be struck by its profane atmosphere. Is there any
theology in the Hebrew tale of Esther? Or putting the question in a different way, is it fair to expect that there should be?

Theology and Esther

Any attempt to answer this point should take into account
the broader wisdom tradition into which Esther fits. Students
of Israelite wisdom literature readily acknowledge that many of
the traditional elements of Jewish piety such as covenant,
election, inheritance, sacrifice, liturgical worship and prayer
hardly feature at all in such writings as Proverbs, Qoheleth and
large sections of Job and Ben Sirach. Instead, there is a focus on
how to cope with life's problems, particularly on how to
survive in the midst of unfair treatment. The secular nature of
the Israelite wisdom tradition however is more apparent than
real, and even though many passages appear to be concerned
with such mundane matters as the art of living well, or political
shrewdness, or even with such trivial affairs as good table
manners, there is a very definite context of faith in which all of
this takes place. Israel was influenced by international wisdom
cross-currents, but did not accept these influences uncritically.
Hence, when we turn to Esther, we are dealing with a story

which bears unmistakable echoes of the broader wisdom tradition.

As already suggested, the plot in Esther may be considered as a variant of a classical wisdom theme: why should an innocent people have to undergo undeserved and capricious ridicule and persecution? And the manner in which this question is confronted is in keeping with certain circles within that same tradition, namely a vehement desire that the evil plotted against them be reversed and fall upon the heads of their enemies. Other wisdom motifs are cleverly interwoven around this basic story line. Among these should be noted the splendour and magnificence of the court scenes, the lavish banquets, and the exotic sounding names of the king's eunuchs (1:10) and administrators (1:14).

Of particular interest in this context of a wisdom folk-tale is the heroine of the story, Esther. Because the key role she plays in saving her people is not by force of numbers but by her own daring and personal resources of character, she illustrates effectively a wisdom theme that appears occasionally in earlier Old Testament writings. In 2 Sam 11:21 reference is made to the killing of Abimelech at Tebez by the resourcefulness of a woman who flings a millstone from the city walls down upon him. This event, which is first recounted in Judg 9:50-54, carries overtones of the scorn attached to being killed by a "weakling," for Abimelech cries out to his armour-bearer, "Draw your sword and kill me, lest it be said of me, 'a woman slew him'" (Judg 9:54). And in 2 Sam 20:14-22 it is the wisdom of a unnamed woman which saves the day, as she persuades the town of Abel-beth-maacah to turn over the rebel Sheba to Joab.

By the time we come to Esther, and even more so in Judith,

this theme has reached full blossoming in the motif of how the entire Jewish community is saved from certain and imminent disaster through the ingenuity and courage of a brave and beautiful woman. This is a particular working out of a more general biblical tenet, that God uses those who are apparently "weak" to confound the strong.

Modern audiences, particularly if they are sensitive to the issues of feminism, will not derive great satisfaction from this kind of polarisation of the sexes as weak and strong. Yet such was the sociological reality of biblical times. Women were to be protected and rescued rather than be active agents of protection and rescue. Consequently, when their initiative and courage brought about the downfall of the enemy, it was all the more reason to celebrate success. And if they were beautiful, and if their strategy involved a clever but prudent use of that beauty, it was even still greater reason to rejoice.

The story of Esther has had a chequered career. It was received enthusiastically in some Jewish circles because of its portrayal of the triumph of Israel, but rejected by others, presumably because of its profane atmosphere and bloodthirsty vengeance. It is the only biblical work not attested to among the Essene community at Qumran. If there was disagreement among Jews about accepting Esther into the official lists of scriptural books at the beginning of the first and second centuries, A.D., there was even greater divergence among the Christian Fathers up until the fourth century. And it is well known that in the sixteenth century Martin Luther encountered particular difficulties with this story, so much so that he wished that it "did not exist at all."

But when the tale of Esther is considered within its own terms, and neither historicised nor politicised, most of the difficulties which readers of earlier centuries had disappear. Once again it can be enjoyed for what it is, a literary master-piece, with a well developed plot, and a highly skilled flair for portraying human emotions and human conflicts, all well sea-soned with a healthy and playful sense of humour.

5

THE BOOK OF JONAH:
A CONFLICT OF WILLS

Jonah is, at heart, a humorous book. Its characters and story are intended to raise a smile on the lips of its hearers — or rather, some of its hearers. For the Book of Jonah is a satire, which means that, although it will entertain those who are in tune with its message, it might anger those who are in disagreement. Its humour might have given the book the power to expose and penetrate some of the mild barriers of prejudice and smugness present in its audience; but for those most embedded in post-exilic nationalism, this brief work undoubtedly seemed to hold devotion, patriotism, and the very God of Israel up to ridicule. In short, the Book of Jonah was in bad taste.

Our reading of the Book of Jonah has changed considerably since it has been generally recognised that it is a work of fiction. Individuals, such as St Gregory of Nazianzus in the fourth century, suspected long ago that it was not historical, but reference to the "sign of Jonah" by Jesus in the gospels (Lk

11:29-32; Mt 12:38-42) made Christians very nervous of questioning its historical worth. In fact, Michelangelo's portrayal of Jonah in the Sistine Chapel — in the central position over the high altar and in a scale much larger than any of the other prophets — would imply that Jonah merited an unquestionable precedence of rank among the company of prophets.

Yet the reader, ancient or modern, might reasonably ask the question, "How does Jonah merit a place among the prophets at all?" Unlike the other prophetic books, the Book of Jonah is not filled with oracles delivered from Yahweh through his prophet, The book is manifestly a narrative, with a unified beginning, middle and end which would have delighted the heart of Aristotle. The Old Testament canon was happy enough to receive stories about prophets, such as the Elijah cycle in First and Second Kings or the snippets to be found in the Books of Isaiah and Jeremiah, but nowhere else does a story about a prophet try to hold its own as a prophetic book. And such a story: a runaway prophet, piscine transport, mass conversion and shady plants that spring up one day and wither the next! There certainly is nothing among the prophetic writings to match this.

The Book of Jonah is among the prophets because that is where the author wanted it to fit.[1] The opening words, "The word of Yahweh came go Jonah the son of Amittai, saying ...," expose the author's intentions at once. The expression ". . . the word of Yahweh came . . ." echoes a prophetic idiom found in the Books of Isaiah, Jeremiah, Ezekiel, Hosea, Joel,

---

[1]Although there would have been no established canon of prophetic writing at the time of the composition of Jonah, the author of Jonah wanted to evoke conventions of prophetic writing which would have been familiar to the original audience.

Micah, Zephaniah, Haggai and Zechariah. And, as if that weren't enough, the author shapes this fictional work around the flesh-and-blood prophet Jonah, son of Amittai, whose name is clearly given in the first words of the story.

The Character of Jonah

In fact, that identification hands the audience the key to the author's intention. What we know about the historical Jonah can be given in a few words found in 2 Kings 14:25-27:

> [King Jeroboam II of Israel] restored the border of Israel from the entrance of Hamath to the Sea of the Plain, according to the word of Yahweh, the God of Israel, which he spoke through his servant Johah, son of Amittai, the prophet from Gath-hepher. For Yahweh saw that the oppression of Israel was very harsh and that there was no one, slave or free, to come to the aid of Israel. Yahweh had not said that he would obliterate the name of Israel from under the skies. And he delivered them through Jeroboam the son of Joash.

At first glance, it may seem that this piece tells us only two things about Jonah which we cannot tell from the Book of Jonah: that he prophesied during the reign of Jeroboam II and that he came from Gath-hepher. But looking at the oracle which is reported indirectly in this passage reveals the reason that Jonah would re-emerge as the central character of the book under consideration.

Prophets in the Old Testament world had certain expectations to live up to. They functioned within the context of a cult which was meant to celebrate Yahweh's selection and protection of his people Israel, a protection which manifested itself in a special relationship between Yahweh and the king. The prophets, being experts at invoking Yahweh's Word for every occasion, would be consulted by the monarch before major military campaigns (cf. 1 Kings 22:1-28) and perhaps on certain other occasions, such as at the New Year Festival when they might give the outlook for the coming year. If it is true that good news never sold newspapers, then it is equally true that bad forecasts never made prophets popular. These prophets tended to give oracles which were reassuring to king and people, predicting a great defeat for the enemies of Israel; and in this, they fit into a pattern established for prophecy all over the ancient near eastern world.

Those familiar with the prophetic writings of the Old Testament might feel uncomfortable with the above description of prophecy, and with good reason. Prophets like Amos and Hosea (both of whom lived in the reign of Jeroboam II) could hardly be styled "reassuring." They were prophets of warning, saying that Yahweh — far from unconditionally protecting his people — would bring about the downfall of the kingdom! And similar statements could be made about most of the Old Testament prophets. Jeremiah hardly got thrown into a pit for flattery, nor did the message of Malachi leave his hearers with a warm glow of security.

But the prophets who had their oracles collected into Old Testament books were the exception, not the rule. Even within these books we can witness the activity of the prophets of pleasantries:

> Thus says Yahweh Sabaoth: "Pay no attention to the words of the prophets prophesying to you, filling you with emptiness! Their own heart's vision they speak, not from the mouth of Yahweh. They proclaim to those who hate me, 'Yahweh speaks:

"The peace of Yahweh is yours."'; and to everyone who lives out
the obstinacy of his own heart, they say, "Nothing bad will come
to you.'" (Jer 23:16-17)

It would seem clear from this, and from other passages in
Jeremiah, that the biblical prophets were in a minority. In fact,
it appears that the biblical prophets were reluctant to use the
usual Hebrew term for prophet, *nabhi*, of themselves lest they
should be grouped together with the unctious visionaries
whose platitudes they found themselves opposing. We continue this distinction when speaking of prophecy in the Old
Testament by referring to the reassuring prophets as "false
prophets," a term unknown to the Old Testament itself. True,
the Old Testament castigated prophets for prophesying lies or
giving oracles for money or saying things which people wanted
to hear; but it accepts that their credentials (whatever about
their performance) as prophets are unassailable. If someone
speaks oracles — be those oracles true or false — that person
is a prophet; prophecy was a function, not an honorific title.

If we keep the expectations put upon prophets in Old
Testament times in mind when we read the passage from the
Second Book of Kings, we can see that Jonah, son of Amittai,
fitted the job description brilliantly. When times were rough
for Israel, Jonah spoke oracles of good news for his king and
nation. He predicted that King Jeroboam's military ventures
would result in the restoration of lost territories to the Northern kingdom, as Jeroboam undoubtedly wanted to hear. It was
the type of oracle which would result in condemnation from a
figure like Jeremiah in a later time. But Jonah receives nothing
but honourable mention from the Second Book of Kings
because of one very important factor: his oracle came true.

So the author of the Book of Jonah had in the historical

figure of Jonah a prophet who foretold good things for his people, not disaster like the more important prophetic figures remembered in the tradition. At the heart of this narrative the author placed a prophet who had delivered the oracle of blessing for Israel and calamity for the enemies of God's People; who was, more than likely, only delighted to do so . . . or so the author of the Book of Jonah would have us believe. Even the name of the prophet had the advantage of humorous incongruity: the name of this forecaster of harsh events for Israel's enemies is the Hebrew word for the gentle dove.

But a story is hardly formed out of one character, even a story as short as that of Jonah. So the author takes Jonah out of his comfortable setting at the court of Jeroboam where he can smugly declaim the fortunes of Israel's enemies and sends him off to Nineveh where he must tell God's enemies of their downfall face to face. And, as the audience might expect, Jonah was not at all pleased with these changes in the terms of his employment.

In themselves, these basic parameters establish the major tension evident in the Book of Jonah: Yahweh wants him to go to Nineveh and Jonah doesn't want to go. It is a tension which occasions two resolutions in the story, the first in terms of the will of Jonah and the second in terms of the will of Yahweh. The first resolution takes place in Jon 1:1-3:3a; the second resolution is to be found in Jon 3:3b- 4:11.

The Author's Portrayal of Characters

Before examining these movements in the story, we should look at the various *dramatis personae* which the author utilises in his narrative. Jonah has already been identified as a figure of religious nationalism, a prophet convinced that Yahweh is as jingoistic about Israel as he is himself. Jonah is treated by the author as a figure to be laughed at, whose attitudes lead him into trouble and who is so tenacious in his convictions that he is condemned forever to a life of disgruntled disappointment. Often such a satirical figure is portrayed as two-dimensional, a cardboard cut-out with no depth to back it up. This is not the case with the portrayal of Jonah: he is a man of deep feeling and his trials produce authentic human reactions with which the audience can identify. This identification of the audience with Jonah provides a vital component of the narrative's ability to challenge attitudes of the hearer which might coincide with those of the pathetic prophet.

Most of the other characters in the story can be grouped together, since they all fulfil the same function and act in the same way. These are the pagans, presumed to be the enemies of Israel and therefore the enemies of Yahweh himself. And the presumption would not be without foundation: Nineveh, the city to which Jonah is sent in the story, was the capital of the empire which would crush Jonah's beloved Israel into oblivion, destroying its cities and deporting its population. A large part of the process of conquest would have involved despoiling the temples and shrines of the conquered nation to provide booty for the gods of the triumphant nation. This was hardly an atmosphere for ecumenism.

Yet the pagans in Jonah are treated most sympathetically. Evil as they may be (is it not their wicked ways which prompt the original mission for Jonah to announce their imminent destruction?), as soon as they receive the slightest indication of what Yahweh wants, they respond with full and generous hearts in sharp contrast to grumbling, begrudging Jonah. In this, they are joined by all the forces of nature: wind and wave, beasts of Nineveh, plant and worm, all respond to the will of Yahweh. A great symphony of response and obedience swells in the narrative of Jonah; only the prophet himself seems to resist joining it.

The pagans in Jonah are flat characters, as befits type characters which are meant to evoke set responses from the audience. It could be presumed by the author that every hearer of this work would have her or his own special brand of prejudice against the idolatrous non-Israelites. But the use of humour and exaggeration transforms these characters and defuses the threats which they might pose to the hearer, much in the same way that an animated cartoon can make us react to otherwise threatening animals, such as lions and alligators, as lovable and benign. Even though the portrayal of the pagans in the book is rather shallow, and none of them receives great individuality, in the end they fare much better in the audience's mind than does the hero of the story.

An unusual feature of the story is that Yahweh himself features as a fully developed character. In some of the other biblical short stories, Yahweh is clearly an active force behind the scenes (as in Ruth or Judith), but only in Jonah does he receive a "speaking part," interacting with another character, revealing the intimacies of his own emotions and reasonings. The Yahweh of Jonah is delightfully anthropomorphic, changing his mind as circumstances demand, enduring the verbal dressing down which he receives from an aggrieved prophet, trying to comfort Jonah and to explain to him in tender terms why even divine wrath needs to be held in check at times. Yet for all of the human details with which the author portrays the

divine, Yahweh remains the sovereign of the universe, the
transcendent lord of nature and of destinies. Only human
freedom remains outside of his control — and, perhaps in
Jonah's case, of his sympathetic comprehension. Yahweh can
fetch Jonah back with storms and great fish, he can get Jonah
to perform the task set for him, but Jonah's anger with Yahweh
does not seem to have been part of the plan; it is something
which Yahweh must question and redirect before he can begin
to deal with it. As audience, we might identify with Jonah, but
Yahweh is the figure which we are more likely to find attrac-
tive, especially since he can so quickly put his powerful attributes to one side in order to deal with a situation with
sympathy and tenderness. The God of the Book of Jonah wears
his transcendence lightly.

First Resolution: The Will of Jonah

The first story movement deals with the conflict between
the will of Yahweh and the will of Jonah; Jonah hears the plan
of Yahweh, and decides that he has better ideas. The plan of
Yahweh is given simply in a few words:

> "Arise, go to the great city of Nineveh, and cry out against it; for
> their evil has come into my presence." (Jon 1:2)

Again, taking the cue from Second Kings, we can say that
nothing would please Jonah more than to cry against the
wickedness of the great city of Nineveh, as long as any crying
could be done at home among friends. But confronting people

with their wickedness was not something which came easily to Jonah, it would seem. Especially if you were one little Israelite in a great big pagan city.

So Jonah did the only sensible thing; he emigrated. The text specifies that "Jonah rose" — which is precisely what Yahweh told him to do — "to escape to Tarshish from the presence of Yahweh" — which is not precisely what Yahweh had in mind (Jon 1:3). It is possible to translate the Hebrew phrase as "from standing before Yahweh," which would imply that Jonah was attempting to flee Yahweh's service rather than his presence. This would make sense to the modern reader, imbued with a belief in the omnipresence of God. In the ancient world, however, there was a greater tendency to see a deity more or less restricted to his own nation and its land, as can be seen in the request of Naaman to Elisha in 2 Kings 5:17-19. So small-minded, religiously nationalistic Jonah had deluded himself into thinking that Yahweh would no longer be able to force a mission upon him if he escaped the confines of Israel; just to make certain, Jonah headed for the farthest point west possible, the city of Tarshish, usually identified with Tartessus in the south of Spain. The humour of the book has begun to infect the narrative in the first three sentences: Jonah not only responds to the call of Yahweh in a manner diametrically opposed to the response of every other Old Testament figure who receives such a call; he also shows how limited his view of Israel's God is by his pathetic attempt to escape.

Escape from the presence of Yahweh becomes the end towards which Jonah's will is determined; Jonah's goal becomes the symbol of his conflict with the plan of Yahweh.

Even at this stage, the audience will wait to see whether Jonah will end up in Tarshish or in Nineveh, whether Jonah's plan or Yahweh's plan is the one to win out.

Jonah, of course, was wrong about the geographic bounds which he put on Yahweh, just as he would later be seen to be in error concerning other limitations which he tried to place on the Deity. Yahweh's command of the forces of tempest and sea, however, is lost on Jonah, who is asleep under the deck. The pagans show their piety, misguided though it be, by invoking their gods for help during this crisis; Jonah, on the other hand, must be called to his prayers by the pagan sailors. Only when the casting of lots reveals that he is at fault does Jonah mention to the pagans that he belongs to the people of Yahweh, although he was at the moment trying to escape Yahweh's presence. The pagan sailors are horrified, but are unwilling to follow Jonah's advice to throw him into the sea to calm the storm. When hard rowing fails to produce any result, they themselves invoke Yahweh (there is no indication that Jonah himself has prayed to Yahweh throughout this entire crisis — piety is left entirely to the pagans) and hesitantly throw their offending passenger into the water. The water becomes calm, and the pagans become devotees of the God of Israel:

> Then the men feared Yahweh to be sure. They sacrificed an offering to Yahweh and made vows. (Jon 1:16).

A further irony may be intended by the locating of these scenes at sea; indeed, Jonah's limited view of Yahweh would have been thoroughly disproved if these events had taken place in a distant land, such as Egypt. But there are indications that *yam*, the Sea, was thought of as a mythical enemy of Yahweh which had to be subdued during the mighty acts of creation (cf. Job 38:8-11). If this overtone is intended, then even Yahweh's former foe and everything in it and on it are combining forces to teach the disobedient prophet his lessons.

Through Jonah's admission of his guilt, the pagans are put into a position very similar to Jonah's own. They saw clearly the will of Yahweh (i.e., that Jonah be thrown overboard). This is in conflict with their own view of the situation, so they attempt their own solution (rowing hard towards the land). When this fails, they go beyond what Jonah has done so far in the narrative and give in to God's plan. When they see how God's plan works for them (the sea becomes calm and the danger is averted), they understand the greatness of Yahweh and worship him with sacrifices and vows.

Jonah's story, however, lags behind that of the sailors. Yahweh sends along the famous fish which becomes Jonah's maritime home for the next three days. The narrative states that Johah prayed in the belly of the fish (Jon 2:1), the first time throughout all of these trials that Jonah is depicted in that activity. The Hebrew text could be read as implying that it was after three days that Jonah began to pray. For a prophet, his devotion is not overwhelming. It is difficult to know which the author intended to be more humorous — the preposterous fish with Jonah sloshing around in its belly, or the idea of how much Jonah had to endure before he began to pray.

The prayer of Jonah which is given in Jon 2:2-9 is generally conceded to be an independent composition inserted into the narrative. Its style and vocabulary are different from the rest of the book, and although it has a maritime theme it makes no mention of Jonah's present condition, stuck in the belly of the fish. This has led some scholars to hold that this psalm did not form part of the original author's version of the story. Indeed, the history of the Book of Esther, as has been seen, shows that later redactors felt free to include the texts of prayers where earlier versions of the story had simply indicated that Esther had prayed, without going into what precisely she had said.

However, the connections which exist between the psalm of Jon 2:2-9 and the narrative section of the book make it more probable that the author placed this prayer in his text from the start, using a prayer which had come down to him in the tradition. The connections underline the thrusts of the narrative and underpin the character of Jonah.

The sea imagery of 2:3 is, in the poem which came into the hands of the author of Jonah, most probably an image for overwhelming affliction, as is evident in Ps 69:1-2 or in Ps 88:7, 16-17. The connection with the first part of the story of Jonah is accidental; yet it provides the link which allows this psalm to be placed in the mouth of the prophet.

When the audience remembers the trouble which Jonah went to in order to escape the presence of Yahweh, they cannot help but smile at the prophet's lament that he is now "cast from your presence" (literally, "from before your eyes" Jon 2:4). Again, the implications of this phrase within the present narrative are somewhat accidental; while Ps 31:22 would indicate that these words simply mean that the psalmist has fallen outside of the scope of Yahweh's beneficence, Jonah is echoing the geographical ideas of Yahweh which first made his flight seem possible. One may, however, presume that those geographical ideas were somewhat modified in light of his tempestuous experience. But restoration is still viewed in terms of coming back to the place where Yahweh is worshipped (Jon 2:4, 7).

A more subtle connection with the larger narrative occurs in Jon 2:7 where Jonah acknowledges that suffering has reminded him of Yahweh. It has taken much suffering indeed to bring the audience from the oblivious Jonah sleeping in the hold of the boat to the fervent Jonah praying in the piscine stomach. But the real place of suffering is something yet to be developed by the narrative into one of the most important aspects of the book.

If the author of Jonah were of two minds whether or not to include this poem, Jon 2:8 would have clinched the argument for inclusion. Through that verse, Jonah can vent his disgust at those who worship "empty idols" (literally, "vanities of emptiness") instead of worshipping the one true God. The psalm ends with the contrasting figure of Jonah who will make his sacrifice of thanksgiving to Yahweh (Jon 2:9). By making this vow, Jonah has finally caught up with the spiritual development of the pagan sailors whom the narrative left three days before.

The humour of the fish is brought to an untidy end in Jon 2:10. Yahweh speaks to the fish which then vomits Jonah up on the dry ground. There is no dignity to this scene. Jonah does not step onto the shore clean and neatly pressed Yahweh's answer to his prayer delivers him, alright, but with a minimum of comfort.

Jonah's goal of Tarshish is now clearly seen as unattainable; Jonah's will is not to have its way. But has the plan of Yahweh really triumphed? The tension which was established in the first words of the story is no closer to resolution. Neither the psalm nor any other part of the narrative so far has indicated that Jonah is going to succumb to the will of Yahweh. True, he is safe and sound in Israel again, so the audience and Jonah have both been brought back, by a very circuitous route, to the point of origin.

So, in a sense, the story begins again in Jon 3:1. The word of Yahweh again is addressed to Jonah, and again Jonah arises. But this time he heads in the right direction, toward Nineveh, the sin capital of the world.

With that verse, the narrative reaches its first major resolution. Jonah's will has been in direct conflict with God's plan. Even though the decisions which Jonah makes are permitted to run their course in part, the prophet discovers that there is no real escape from the plan of Yahweh. However, the audience has seen enough of the prophet to know that his heart is not really in the mission. Wind and sea and fish can conspire with Yahweh to set Jonah's feet in the right direction, but it will take far more than that to get his heart to follow.

The Second Resolution: The Will of Yahweh

The tension which lay behind the first resolution of the story was stated by the author in the first few verses of the book. The second resolution, which runs from Jon 3:3b to the end of the book, also begins with an indication of the tension.

> Nineveh was a powerful city; it took three days to cross it. Jonah started to enter the city — only one day's journey — and he cried out and said, "Forty days more and Nineveh will be destroyed."

The tension is not readily apparent in most english translations. The phrase which is translated "Nineveh was a powerful big city . . ." reads in the Hebrew *w^{e}nîn^{e}wê hay^{e}thâ 'îr-g^{e}dhôlâ lêlohîm*, "And Nineveh was a city great to God." Although the expression in this form is unique in the Hebrew Bible, linking terms with *'^{e}lohîm*, "God," was an idiomatic way of connoting greatness and majesty. This is why certain translations will render what moved upon the face of the waters in Gen 1:2 as "the Spirit of God" (which sounds appropriately theological) while others will read "a mighty wind" (which is rather more mundane). Both sets of translators are staring at the same Hebrew words; but they make different decisions about the way that *'^{e}lohîm* is being used in the sentence.

Undoubtedly the Book of Jonah intends to tell us that Nineveh is an exceedingly great city, with the added humorous exaggeration of a three day journey to cross it. But the statement that the city was great to God is also important, for therein lie the seeds of the second tension: how can Yahweh destroy the city which is so great to him? This conflict within the character of Yahweh himself provides the backdrop for the rest of the drama.

But back to Jonah himself. Just as his devotion has failed to overwhelm us, so his communication techniques strike us as somewhat primitive. His message is simple and direct, but it hardly complies with the pattern set by the canonical prophets; many of them also prophesied destruction for their hearers, but often with exhortations to correct what was wrong in order to avert the catastrophe. Jonah, on the other hand, simply announces the destruction and the date as a *fait accompli*.

Jonah is presuming that repentance is out of the question. If Hebrew prophets told their audiences to repent, they often used the word *sûbh* which means "return." They begged their people to return to God, to return to the covenant, to return to

the ways of justice and communal responsibility which lay at
the roots of their nation. But how could Jonah tell a pagan city
to "return"? These people had never known Yahweh, had
always worshipped idols, and Jonah would have been quite
certain that Ninevites had been wicked from the first days of
the city's foundation.

If memories of the pagan sailors in the first part of the story
warn us about what the Ninevites will do, the Ninevite reaction seems to take Jonah by surprise. Jonah is only a third of
the way through the city when the impossible happens. Sackcloth and ashes are the order of the day, from the king down to
the herds and flocks. The solemn statement of Abram's faith in
Gen 15:6 is echoed again in Jon 3:5, the people of Nineveh
"put their trust in God," and the king of Nineveh makes the
decree which the prophet has failed to make, "let every one
turn from his evil way and from the oppression done by his
hands." (Jon 3:8) The prophetic word *sûbb* has found its way
into the book at last, even if it will not come from the lips of
the prophet himself.

In the first part of the book, Jonah's plans were tending
toward a goal which was never to be reached, the far-off city of
Tarshish. But now, Yahweh's plans have also stumbled at an
obstacle; the repentance of Nineveh means that the destruction
which God had planned was never to materialise. In one of the
most outstanding anthropomorphic strokes of the Old Testament, God repents of the evil that he had made Jonah
announce.

In this way, the tension which was implied at the beginning
of this second section reaches some kind of resolution. Yahweh's plans for the destruction of Nineveh went against his

regard for the city itself. The action of the Ninevites, prompted by the message of Jonah, have allowed Yahweh's greater will — the survival of the Ninevites — to triumph over the demands of justice.

The book could have ended there, and some of the older interpretations of the book nearly seemed to have thought that it did. For some interpreters of recent times, the main point of the book was to satirise the lack of response on the part of Israel to their many heroic prophets by contrasting it with a pagan response to a rather less than ideal prophet. Thus the Book of Jonah became for them a propaganda tract to ward off the rampant nationalism of the post-exilic period.

It would be very foolish to deny that the Book of Jonah goes out of its way to speak well of the pagans, or that it came to be written after the exile was ended. Yet the real message of the book cannot be discerned until the whole story is told; and for that we definitely need what is in the fourth chapter.

The third chapter does sound like an ending, and a very happy ending too. Jonah was sent to decry the evil of Nineveh and, with one or two mishaps along the way, he does just that; the Ninevites respond with prayer and fasting, and God decides that Nineveh can survive after all. So God is happy, the Ninevites are happy, and — presumably — Jonah is happy. As a prophet, he has been such a runaway success that an Ezekiel or a Jeremiah might be envious.

Instead, we are presented with a very different picture:

> Things were going badly for Jonah, very badly indeed, and he was raging! He begged Yahweh, "Oh, I implore, Yahweh, was this not what I said while I was in my own land? That is why I went out to run away to Tarshish, for I knew 'You are God,

gracious and merciful — slow to anger and vast in loving kindness and a lamenter of evil.' And now, Yahweh, please take my life from me, for my death would be better than my life." (Jon 4:1-3)

The character of Jonah, somewhat neglected since Jon 3:4, re-emerges in the narrative to show that the tension is not resolved to everyone's satisfaction. Before the story can have the happy ending to which it is unquestionably headed, one major figure has to be consoled.

Jonah's anger is consistent with his portrayal as a hater of pagans. But it is also fueled by his public loss of face. In any event, there is only one way in which this story will have a happy ending in Jonah's eyes: the whole three-day-wide cosmopolitan area of Nineveh will have to go up in flames according to schedule, just as Jonah announced. So Jonah, having gone to great lengths to conform with what Yahweh asked him to do, finds himself once more in conflict with the will of God. This time, he is no longer willing to yield under pressure. He just wants to die.

The final act of the drama (Jon 4:1-11), which describes this clash between Jonah's will and Yahweh's decision, falls into two parts, or short scenes. The first, Jon 4:1-4, gives the immediate response of the prophet to the disappointing news that Nineveh would be spared. The second scene, Jon 4:5-11, shows us Jonah waiting against hope that his will might be done after all. And, as the reader might expect when wills are so obviously in conflict, both scenes contain a defence of the stance taken by each of the protagonists.

Jonah makes the defence of his own position, tinged with accusation against Yahweh. He justifies his former attempt to avoid the mission on the grounds that he knew that Yahweh would not have the courage to carry out his threats. The majestic attributes of Ex 34:6-7 and the tender description of Joel 2:13 now become bitter words which promise only disappointment to those who rely on Yahweh to be the vindictive punisher of evil that Jonah wants. Yahweh may be under the illusion that he had changed his mind and repented of the evil he had resolved to do, but Jonah had him pegged all along: Jonah knew Yahweh better than Yahweh knew himself.

This conflict of wills results in Jonah's anger, an anger that prefers death to life. Indeed, Jonah prays for death, pronouncing that the good of his death exceeds the good of his life. Yahweh answers his prayer only with a question, asking what is the good of his anger. It is a gentle question, a caring response which once more highlights the gulf between Yahweh's personality and Jonah's. The almighty Yahweh, who controls the winds and seas and fish, who dictates the fate of powerful cities, is most truly himself in this caring gentleness; far from being the god of wrath that Jonah would have liked to serve, Yahweh questions the very presence of anger in his servant. Flaring rage belongs not to him, but to the uncaring, unfeeling, and ultimately powerless Jonah, to the prophet who knows all about God, who can predict divine actions better than the Deity himself, and who cannot understand him one whit.

Despite all appearances, despite what the prophet himself proclaimed in his little speech, Jonah heads out "till he should see what would become of the city." He builds a temporary shelter hoping that at the end of the forty day period he might yet witness the destruction which he had foretold. He hasn't really given up hope at all; Jonah sits waiting for his will to be done.

In his final scene, Yahweh justifies his actions to Jonah,

having heard the accusations which the prophet makes against him. The forces of nature are once more raised against the rebellious prophet, albeit in a much gentler way than before.

The first part of the demonstration consisted of a plant to give Jonah some shade while he sits in his patchwork hut watching for the city's destruction. And Jonah, angry though he is, can still appreciate the plant's shade in the Mesopotamian heat; he was "absolutely thrilled with the castor-oil plant." (Jon 4:6).

But the plant was only part one of the demonstration. Part two (next morning — Yahweh wastes no time) was a worm to destroy the plant before dawn and part three was the burning east wind, the sirocco full of dust and heat, which made life rather unpleasant in a hut waiting for a city to be destroyed. The final straw was the sun which was doing to Jonah's head what the worm did to his plant (the same verb is used for both). But the demonstration does not seem to have been very effective; it results in the same prayer for death which we heard before it began at all.

We have seen that there is much conscious evocation of the prophetic literature in the Book of Jonah, and this prayer of Jonah provides one more example. The model for his prayer is the mighty figure of Elijah after he had been informed that Jezebel had declared his life forfeit.

> Then he was afraid, and he got up and ran for his life. He arrived at Beer-sheba in the territory of Judah, and made his servant stay there. He himself went a day's journey into the desert, and came and sat under a lone broom tree. He asked that his life turn to death and said, "Too much now, Yahweh! Take my life — I am no better than my ancestors." (1 Kings 19:3-4).

Elijah, too, had to undergo a catechesis. He complained that he alone was left after a massive apostasy by Israel (1 Kings 19:10). The demonstration for Elijah consisted in a theophany on the very mountain of God, Horeb in Sinai. A mighty wind, an earthquake, a raging fire — all sometime symbols of Yahweh's commanding presence — passed before Elijah on the mountain of God; but all were devoid of the presence of Yahweh. God was only to be found in a "still, small voice" (1 Kings 19:12). And after Yahweh had made Elijah see how wrong he could be about what a proper theophany should be, he let the prophet know that he was equally wrong about being the lone Yahwish left; Elijah had missed seven thousand in his reckoning (1 Kings 19:18).

As in the case of his forebear Elijah, Jonah's lesson is completed by a response from Yahweh. Yahweh's question about the validity of Jonah's anger is seemingly repeated in 4:9, but there is a difference: "Does your anger over the castor-oil plant do any good?" Before this, Jonah's anger was too general to be discussed; he was angry over Nineveh, enraged with God, embarrassed that his prophecy to all these people that they would be destroyed went unfulfilled, fed up with his prophetic vocation — where could Yahweh begin to address all the issues involved? But now that the anger was narrowed down to the destruction of a plant, a rational response could be attempted. The demonstration had achieved that much.

Loveless Jonah had made his fatal mistake by caring about a plant. It wasn't much, but it was enough to allow Yahweh to begin speaking to Jonah in terms of the language of divine concern. Yahweh points out to Jonah that, in fact, he had little reason to care about the plant at all; the plant came and went regardless of Jonah who had no responsibility for its welfare. If Jonah could feel such anger when a plant withered, what was Yahweh supposed to feel when the existence of so many human persons was at stake, people who could not really be held liable to the death that their sins might seem to merit; for in truth they are people "who cannot tell their right hand from their left, and" — in the final rub of this didactic jest — "there are a great many cattle, too." (Jon 4:11).

In this final stage of resolution, the second tension also has shown itself to be a tension between the will of Yahweh and the will of Jonah. In the first tension, Jonah was at odds with Yahweh's plans concerning the prophet himself and his destiny; now, in this second tension, Jonah disagrees with the ways in which Yahweh handles the affairs of the Gentiles. Jonah protests in anger that the two tensions are in fact interconnected (Jon 4:2), and even though the audience might suspect that the prophet's flight had less foresight than he claimed for it, we would have little doubt that Jonah's inability to come to terms with Yahweh's decisions has one cause in its two manifestations: Jonah has made himself too small to absorb the great designs of Yahweh.

But what of this ending: is it really a fully satisfactory resolution of the tensions which the narrative has evoked? Before adddressing that question, a brief glance at the narrative of Jonah from a different perspective is in order.

How to Teach a Theologian about God

So far, the Book of Jonah has been treated in terms of two great resolutions resulting from narrative tensions. Those responsible for dividing the book into chapters have noticed another possibility for sectioning the story; put into a very simplified form, it could be summarised thus:

Chapter One: The first call and subsequent events.
Chapter Two: The prayer of Jonah and Yahweh's response.
Chapter Three: The second call and subsequent events.
Chapter Four: The prayer of Jonah and Yahweh's response.

This fourfold division readily reduces itself to a diptych, Part One consisting of chapters one and two, Part Two of chapters three and four. Closer examination reveals that each of these parts has many structural similarities to its neighbour, producing the general pattern: *call, response of Jonah, conversion of the pagans, suffering and prayer of Jonah, response of Yahweh.*

These two ways of dividing the book — either according to the two calls or according to the two great resolutions — are not mutually exclusive. They are both to be found in the text of the book itself, and their overlapping tends to strengthen the general structure of the story in the same way that staggered rows of brick strengthen a wall.

The *call of Yahweh* which is similar in both parts is followed by the *response of Jonah* which is markedly different in each part. In Part One, the flight to Tarshish represents an absolute rebellion by the prophet; in Part Two, there is outward compliance in Jonah's actions.

No matter what Jonah's action happens to be, it is followed by a *conversion of the pagans.* This, too, follows its own pattern: the pagans are in ignorance and sin (the sailors are active in idolatry, the wickedness of the Ninevites is stated in more generic terms), Jonah speaks to them as a prophet, and they react in complete conformity to God's will. Commentators rightly point out that this pattern represents a satirical contrast with the reception that the great prophets of Israel received from God's own people.

The *suffering and prayer of Jonah* is another section which differs greatly between the two parts. In Part One, the prayer takes the form of an (older) psalm. It stems from Jonah's suffering and acknowledges God's power in Jonah's present situation and begs for life. In Part Two, the prayer begins from Jonah's suffering, is interspersed with more suffering, and begs for death. The prayer for life implies that Jonah is ready to be reconciled with the will of God. The prayer for death shows that Jonah is no longer willing to compromise with God and his ways; having seen how Yahweh runs his world, Jonah prefers annihilation to continued existence in the shadow of divine caprice.

The *response of Yahweh* corresponds to the prayer of Jonah. His response to the prayer for life may be messy, but it is positive. The response to the prayer for death is far less simple. Rather than giving an outright refusal, Yahweh goes to great lengths to show why the prayer is grounded in all of the wrong reasons; in doing so, Yahweh is also trying to communicate to the prophet an understanding of his dealings with Nineveh.

The similar function of suffering in both Parts One and Two is striking; it is only through suffering that Jonah, so bent on going along paths directly opposed to Yahweh's plans, can be made to think again. It is only in suffering that Jonah turns to Yahweh. Even though Jonah knows all about God, can give Yahweh's message to the pagans, can even dare to tell Yahweh all about himself, only suffering has a chance of making Jonah sympathise with the way that Yahweh runs his world. Perhaps the real satire of the book is that a half-hearted prophet can convert Sin City in a day's bad preaching; but God has to mobilise half of the forces of creation to teach his prophet anything.

If suffering poses a problem for Christians today, it posed even more of a problem to the people of Old Testament times. Before there was any concept that God would reward the just and punish the wicked in the life to come, it was patently obvious that he should do it here and now. Suffering was therefore something reserved for the wicked; if good people suffered, it was a temporary measure to correct a fault (as in Ps 119:67 or Ps 32). Religious people may have pondered the problem of suffering, but there was no real mystery to it; the function of suffering in the divine plan for humanity was predictable, a mechanical corrective to imbalances in the human cosmos.

To the author of the Book of Jonah, however, suffering had greater potential. The main character of the book is painted as a comic hero, and comic heroes are expected to suffer; slapstick remains the first language of humour. But the suffering of Jonah is not gratuitous. The suffering in Part One might be construed as a just and effective corrective to Jonah's misguided flight, but the same construct can hardly be applied to Part Two. Jonah has fulfilled the commandment placed upon him, and still he suffers; in fact, his suffering is far deeper, for it provokes an anger that cries out for death.

The suffering of Jonah in both parts of the book enables the prophet to see what God is about. Jonah's suffering in the stomach of the fish — where he was only concerned about his own survival — was enough to make him conform to Yahweh's call. Both the suffering and the response had a certain

superficiality. But Jonah's suffering as he watched for Nineveh
to be destroyed allowed a new element to enter in: concern for
a plant. Perhaps the concern was not very deep; perhaps it
could never have developed into a meaningful relationship . . .
it was, after all, more a concern for shade than for the plant.
But a love which is deep enough to allow suffering is a love
that Yahweh can use to explain his own position in his dealings
with humanity. Jonah learned nothing through his visions and
oracles; even though he could boast of being Yahweh's prophet
and quote the Scriptures, only his love for a withered plant
constituted some sort of common ground between himself and
his God.

Now we are in a position to consider the ending. If the
overriding tensions of the Book of Jonah are between the will
of Yahweh and the will of Jonah, does this final speech of
Yahweh really settle anything? Did Jonah respond by becoming a good prophet, loving all of the pagans as God himself did,
telling them what to do to become decent people? Or did he
grow old as he watched over the city, brooding over it and
nursing his macabre hope? Why does Jonah disappear from
the story at this vital point?

The truth is, Jonah's disappearance is the final statement of
his utter contingency. Throughout the narrative, we have witnessed the overriding power of God's will and the absolute
ineffectiveness of Jonah's, even though Jonah's centrality to the
story may have masked this somewhat. At the end of the story,
we know that Jonah's response to Yahweh will make no
difference: Yahweh will not be swayed from his generous
decision by Jonah's anger. Jonah's dangerous designs for the
pagan city have been defused in the narrative; only the abiding

love of Yahweh for all peoples — Israelite or pagan — remains. This is all that was ever important in the story anyway.

The disappearance of Jonah has another function as well. The final question of Yahweh demands an answer, but Jonah is no longer there to give it. The audience discovers that the question must be answered by them; the answer that Jonah would give is no longer seen as important — it is the response which the audience decides upon which makes the story a happy one or a tragic failure.

Jonah has demonstrated how ridiculous and painful it is to resist the plan of Yahweh. The narrative has used him to warn religious people against becoming like him, locked in a closed cramped religiosity of his own making and angry that God refuses to come and be locked in too. We are warned against viewing humanity in ways that imply that God is only really concerned with some, or that his justice should strike others down in flames. We are warned that sometimes we become so smug that Yahweh can only speak to us when our love turns to suffering.

Jonah was undeniably a theologian. His mastery of the theory was complete. Even when Yahweh did the unannounced, Jonah could trace the trajectory of the action from solid theological grounds. Undoubtedly Jonah had framed a theology of nationalism and divine retribution which was reasonable, comprehensible and comfortable; but Jonah still found his God to be ultimately unreasonable, incomprehensible, uncomfortable. Those who read the Book of Jonah, feeling that they have all of the answers, are reminded that God might still pose some problems that they had not considered before.

6

THE BOOK OF TOBIT:
THE PATTERN OF MERCY

As soon as scholars try to establish the basic text of Tobit, they come up against overwhelming evidence that it is a traditional narrative. The Greek text comes down to us in three recensions; St Jerome's Latin version may be based on a fourth recension which is no longer in existence, and fragments of the book in Hebrew and Aramaic, found among the Dead Sea scrolls, do little to simplify the problem.[1] There is even no certainty whether the book was originally composed in Greek, Aramaic or Hebrew, although scholars tend to favour an original in a Semitic language. In all of this, the Book of Tobit shows that it was not the product of a single creative storyteller, but a work which was changed by its transmitters as their common property.

[1]Different translations follow different recensions of the book. The translation and verse divisions in this chapter follow the text which is found in the Codex Vaticanus and Codex Alexandrinus (as edited by Alfred Rahlfs), and might differ at times from the translation which the reader may be using.

Some of the influences evident in the framing of the story clearly belong to the realm of folklore. The legend of Ahiqar, an ancient hero who appears in many traditions, has made an impact on the teaching of the book — and Ahiqar himself appears as one of its characters. Other aspects of the story — such as Tobit's burial of the dead, the help from a supernatural agent, and Sarah's misfortune with her husbands — have also been traced back to their possible connections with folklore. The book represents a reweaving of material which had been ratified by communal transmission; but an examination of the work predominantly in terms of its sources could be misleading, for the Book of Tobit moves the teachings of the traditions on to new applications and toward a new conclusion which represents the unique vision of its storyteller.

Tobit and the Wisdom Outlook

One of the most influential sources of inspiration for the Book of Tobit comes from the Old Testament itself. The person who framed the story is aware of the main bodies of canonical literature — Torah, prophets and wisdom — and incorporates clear references to these writings in the finished narrative: both the personal sorrow of Tobit and the eventual vindication of God's people happen in accordance with prophetic utterance (Tob 2:6, 14:4-5), and reference is made to both customs and characters to be found in the books of the Law (Tob 1:6, 10-12, 4:12; 6:13; 8:6). However, the strongest impact evident in Tobit seems to have been made by the wisdom tradition.

The major books of the wisdom tradition in the Hebrew canon of Scripture are easy enough to identify: Proverbs, Job,

Qoheleth; the Greek canon would make the important additions of Sirach and the Wisdom of Solomon. Yet the wisdom tradition was larger than these books might indicate. Naturally, an important source of wisdom was the traditional advice handed down from one generation to another — the rules of thumb, the pithy proverbs, the wise observations born from experience. But there was a more sophisticated art of wisdom which belonged to the specialists such as scribes, courtly advisers and teachers of wisdom. This latter strain of wisdom is sometimes referred to as an international intellectual movement which transcended cultural and even religious boundaries. Its task was to identify the proper way to govern one's life, or even one's nation, so that success and tranquillity would be assured. Sometimes wisdom investigated the major problems of life, notably the suffering of the righteous, the meaning of death, and the various limitations of human knowledge and action.

As mentioned in the treatment of Esther, the earlier strains of wisdom literature found in the Old Testament can sound quite secular to the modern ear. There is scant mention of God in large tracts of Proverbs, for instance, and everything seems geared to "getting on" in life. This quality of the earlier wisdom literature is in keeping with the international nature of the wisdom movement: its mobility between nations and peoples, each with their own deities, tended to mean that wisdom's concern with local religious traditions and beliefs was kept to a minimum. But, as wisdom took root in Israel, it continuously drew more and more of its inspiration and imagery from the ancient faith of that people, and the secular tone of wisdom became less and less prominent in later works, such as the Wisdom of Solomon.

Most of these characteristics of wisdom literature have left an imprint on the Book of Tobit. The traditional advice which passed from one generation to another is well represented by the fourth chapter of Tobit, wherein Tobit gives Tobias instructions, not just for the journey ahead, but for life;[2] large portions of that chapter, at least in its longer recension, could be happily transported into a work such as Proverbs without much violence being done to it. As for the courtly, specialist tradition of wisdom — the heart of the wisdom movement — it too is invoked by the narrative of Tobit; for Tobit himself is an official at court (Tob 1:13), the precise type of person who would have been associated with the teachings of wisdom.

The larger problems of life also concern the author of Tobit. In one sense, the book takes up the same situation that intrigued the framers of the story of Job: here, too, the audience is shown a perfectly righteous person, head and shoulders above the rest of his generation, who is suddenly and inexplicably smitten with misfortune. But the problem is doubled in Tobit, for the same type of unexplainable anguish afflicts Sarah who has buried seven husbands on seven wedding nights only to endure the mockery of her maidservants. Although the Book of Tobit does not investigate the problem of suffering as does the Book of Job or the Wisdom of Solomon, the reality of the problem provides Tobit with its major narrative tensions, as shall be seen.

Even a first reading of the book reveals a concern with almsgiving: Tobit mentions his acts of charity in the land of his exile (1:16-17), immediately thinks of the poor in the

[2]The advice of a father to his son was a literary fiction often employed in wisdom literature. Its use in the Old Testament wisdom literature can be found in such places as Prov 1:8-19 and Sir 2:1-6.

midst of abundance (2:2), impresses upon his son the importance of almsgiving (4:7-11, 16-17), and demonstrates his generosity in his decision concerning the reimbursement of Raphael (12:4-5), who in turn confirms the benefits of almsgiving (12:8-9). The final words of Tobit reinforce the theme. "So now, children, see what almsgiving does and how uprightness saves" (14:11).

Perhaps the giving of alms is part and parcel of religious practice today, but the earlier traditions of the Old Testament made little mention of it for their time. The first texts which speak of almsgiving (as distinct from the provision of measures to enable the underprivileged to sustain themselves or prophetic demands for social justice) come from the wisdom tradition:

> The person with a generous eye will be blessed,
>   for he gives some of his bread to the poor. (Prov 22:9)

> There is no want for the person who gives to the poor;
>   there are many curses for the person who shields the eyes.
> (Prov 28:27)

The later wisdom book of Sirach also set forth the ideal of almsgiving:

> Water puts out a spreading fire;
>   and almsgiving atones for sins.
> Whoever repays favours is mindful of things to come,
>   and at the time of collapse will find a firm support.
>   (Sir 3:30-31)

The wisdom tradition has provided the Book of Tobit with one of its connecting themes: that the giving of alms will not go unrewarded. Tobit, who assiduously follows the wisdom teaching concerning generosity to the poor and who hands on that tradition to his son, is eventually rewarded for his faithfulness against overwhelming odds.

Strange as it may seem, the wisdom tradition even enters the stage of Tobit as a character with somewhat more than a walk-on part. Mention has already been made of the story of Ahiqar which seems to serve as one of the sources for the Book of Tobit. The story concerns a devout and wise official to the king of Assyria; he was childless and so adopted his nephew Nadab as his son and heir. He instructs Nadab in the ways of wisdom, but Nadab is of an evil heart, and brings to the king false accusations against Ahiqar, which he succeeds in making plausible. As a result, Ahiqar is condemned to death, but manages to survive, hidden away for years, until events make the king realise his mistake. Ahiqar then reveals himself, and punishes Nadab with methods suitable for such an enduring tale. The legend of Ahiqar has survived in various forms, including a reworking in the legend of Aesop and a retelling in the Arabian Nights. In fact, as far as folklore goes, it would seem that only Solomon keeps Ahiqar from taking most of the kudos for wisdom.

And then, when we turn to the Book of Tobit, what do we find? Here is Ahiqar as the nephew of Tobit himself! Ahiqar does not speak one word in the narrative, contrary to what we might expect. Instead, he makes four brief, but interesting, appearances. In the first one (Tob 1:21-22), Tobit had left home to escape the capital sentence pronounced upon him, but Ahiqar's intervention enabled Tobit to return home in safety. In the second (Tob 2:10), after the tragedy of accidental blindness afflicted Tobit, Ahiqar took care of him. Ahiqar disappears from the narrative until 11:19 when his presence is noted at the festivities which mark the successful conclusion of Tobit and Tobias' adventures. And finally, Tobit mentions the vindication of Ahiqar's wisdom in almsgiving as an example to his family as he makes his deathbed speech (Tob 14:10).

Ahiqar is more than a footnote to add to Tobit's prestige; he is a narrative reminder of the help and consolation offered to the afflicted person by wisdom, a wisdom which will also see the story through to the happy ending for all who endure. And, as might be expected in the context of Tobit, the highest expression of wisdom in action (as exemplified by Ahiqar himself) is care for the unfortunate and the giving of alms.

It would be erroneous to situate Tobit unequivocally within the wisdom literature of the Old Testament, ranking it with such specialist literary works as Job, Qoheleth and Sirach. But much of Tobit is certainly guided by wisdom concerns, and the narrative explicitly acknowledges its debt to wisdom tradition. If Tobit is seen as a product of the wisdom movement, it must be at a very popular level; and the narrative form is a key element in the facilitation of that popularisation.

Introduction of the Character of Tobit

From the opening chapter, the Book of Tobit draws us into a world decorated with a veneer of historical fragments but constructed from the outlook of the original storyteller and of his tradition. A superficial glance might lead us to be impressed by the veneer as the storyteller invokes such important periods of Israel's history as the divided kingdom, the fall of Samaria and the deportation of the northern tribes; but these are simply narrative props which aid the audience in understanding the type of character that Tobit is and in sympathising with his story. If the details of Tobit's early life as recorded in this chapter were taken seriously, Tobit would be about the age of two hundred and thirty before his adventures as narrated in the book even began!

Yet there is something of vital interest in this chapter: Tobit was not part of the schism of the northern tribes which resulted in the divided kingdom (1:6). This schism was not only of a political nature, but had religious implications as well. It meant that the northern tribes deserted the Jerusalem Temple (which had come to be seen as the *only* place where Yahweh could be worshipped according to the liturgy prescribed in Torah) and established their own temples at Dan and Bethel, idolatrous worship in the eyes of the Yahwism of Judah, the southern kingdom (1 Kings 12:25-33; Tob 1:5). In fact, according to the theological viewpoint of the south, the terrible fate of the northern tribes — deportation and eventual loss of identity — is judged to be the direct result of their unfaithful worship (cf. 2 Kings 17:6-23). In stressing that he alone from the northern tribes went to the Jeruasalem temple to worship, Tobit subtly depicts himself as the totally innocent victim of the sins of his nation, "taken captive to Nineveh" (1:10) despite his blameless behaviour.

The confession of virtue which introduces the adventures of Tobit is found in Tob 1:3-9; although the fidelity of Tobit to the Jerusalem Temple is the centrepiece, it is framed by the virtue of almsgiving (1:3) and the practice of the marriage to a kinswoman (1:9), both moral lessons which the storyteller wishes to communicate to his audience throughout the narrative of Tobit's adventures. These verses seem to be uneconomic from the narrative point of view, for they apparently add no meaningful detail to the portrayal of Tobit which we do not have elsewhere in the book, nor do they supply the story movement with either impetus or prop. It is only when we come to investigate the ending of the book that the importance of this handful of verses can truly be seen.

The portrayal of Tobit in 1:10-22 is reminiscent of the picture of Daniel in the book that bears his name. Both are wisdom figures, officials in the service of mighty kings (Dan 1:19-21; Tob 1:1-13). Both refuse to contaminate themselves with unclean food (Dan 1:8-9; Tob 1:10-12). Eventually the virtue of both brings them into violation of the law, with a resultant capital sentence (which fails to be executed in both cases: Dan 6:2-26; Tob 1:18-21).

Overall, Tobit is a person worthy of his name, a symbolic name meaning "My good [is Yahweh]," and it is the intention of these opening verses to leave the audience in no doubt that such is the case. He is shown to us as a person who keeps the Law, who follows ancestral custom, and who is a sage. He persists in his virtuous actions towards his people, even when they endanger him, and he earns the respect of the pagans among whom he must dwell. No matter what befell him, Tobit remained faithful and "remembered God in [his] whole life" (1:12). Once the audience is clearly informed about the character of Tobit, the adventures can begin.

The Establishment of the First Tension: Tobit is Moved to Pray for Death

The story proper begins in 2:1 at the Feast of Weeks (or Pentecost). According to the Deuteronomic description of this feast, it was to be one of rejoicing in the Temple and the disadvantaged (i.e., the alien, the orphan and the widow) were to be invited to the feast (Deut 16:9-12). As the audience would expect, Tobit attempts to comply with the spirit of this command by sending his son Tobias to find a poor Israelite to partake of his festival dinner (2:2); but this good intention lacks a happy conclusion, for Tobias reports that an Israelite has been killed and lies unburied in the market place. True to the pattern outlined in the introduction (1:17-19), Tobit takes it upon himself to give the corpse a burial. The implication of Tobit's care to conceal the corpse (2:4) and of the neighbours' reaction (2:8) is that the ignominious death of the Israelite was an official execution; by his act of kindness, Tobit is once more risking the death sentence.

The storyteller highlights the significance of this event by an invocation of Amos 8:10, showing that the attitude to prophecy at work in the book is one of past prediction and later fulfilment. This use of prophecy will be apparent again in the concluding passages of the work. Tobit's grief here is purely as a member of his people, and the prophecy is taken as programmatic of those woes; Tobit's more personal affliction is only on the horizon at this stage of the narrative.

Since contact with a corpse meant a period of ritual impurity, Tobit spent the following night sleeping in the courtyard of his house. His blindness, which is his central affliction in terms of the narrative, is therefore a direct result of his heroic concern for his people; perhaps the storyteller uses the cause of bird-droppings to emphasise the gratuitous nature of Tobit's misfortune. Since nothing which Tobit has done so far in this narrative is deserving of anything but praise, Tobit becomes a type of Job-figure; all of Tobit's suffering — firstly in his exile, secondly in his flight from a capital sentence, and thirdly in his blindness — occurs despite his innocence and virtue. However, while Job remains innocent throughout his suffering, Tobit has one lapse when he falsely accuses his wife of stealing (2:11-14). Her retort brings into question the wisdom of his former acts of kindness, demonstrating that the first tension is now complete in its construction: virtuous living has seemed to have earned for Tobit only a harvest of misfortune and suffering, as epitomised by his blindness.

Tobit only sees one desirable end to his abundance of sorrows: the mercy of God could now show itself most clearly in allowing Tobit to die soon, and to this end he addresses his prayer.

> 'You are righteous, Lord,
> and all of your works and all of your ways are merciful deeds
>   and truth.
> You give an honest and righteous judgement forever.
> Remember me and look down toward me.
> Do not punish my sins and my unknown offences
> and those of my ancestors which they committed against you,
> for they refused to listen to your commandments.
> You gave us over for abduction, captivity and death, and as a
>   symbol
> of shame to all the nations among whom we are scattered.
>
> And now, your many judgements against me are right to proceed
>   in accordance with my sins and those of my ancestors,
> because we have not performed your commandments,
> for we have not walked faithfully before you.
>
> So now, do with me according to your good pleasure.
> Command that my spirit ascend,
> so that I may depart and become soil,

for it profits me more to die than to live.
I have heard false insults and sorrow is great within me.
Command that I be released at once from my calamity and
    brought to the eternal place.
Do not turn your face from me.' (3:2-6)

Several key elements of the book up to this point are to be found in the prayer. God's acts are characterised as *elēmosynai*, translated above as "merciful deeds" but also the usual word for almsgiving. Tobit (unlike Job) does not protest his innocence, but accepts that his present affliction is a participation in the just punishment for his people's sins as mentioned in 1:4-5, as well as for his personal sins, known and unknown. The plaintive cry of Jon 4:3 is echoed in Tobit's plea for death as an act of mercy.

From this point on, the story moves outside of the realm of Tobit's knowledge and so the first person narration is abandoned. Some have seen the abrupt change of narrative viewpoint as an indication of different sources at work in the text, but this is unnecessary. Inconsistent narrative viewpoints would have been familiar to the storyteller from such works as the Book of Jeremiah, and the deliberate imitation of this technique cannot be totally ruled out.[3]

[3]The opening words of the book ("The book of the words of Tobit son of Tobiel . . .") might be in deliberate imitation of the opening verses of books like that of Jeremiah, giving the figure of Tobit stature like the great prophets according to the understanding of prophecy evident in the work.

The Contrapuntal Tension

The story of Tobit involves a double plot, which necessitates that a second tension — seemingly unrelated to the tension already depicted — be established. The choice of a double plot will eventually mean that these two tensions interact toward their respective resolutions. The connection between the plight of Tobit and the sad tale of Sarah in faraway Ecbatana is drawn by the simple phrase "on that very same day" (3:7) which introduces Sarah's story.

While the trials and tribulations of Tobit are located in the natural order of things, Sarah's problems transport us into a plane of existence where demons afflict innocent young women on their wedding nights, where the supernatural and the human mingle either for good or for evil. It comes as no surprise that Sarah's affliction can be traced to folklore motifs dating back at least as far as Egypt in the fifth century B.C. The story will remain in the realm of the demonic and angelic until the double resolution is complete.

In some ways, Sarah's afflictions parallel those of Tobit: she suffers reproach from those whom society would expect to offer respect (3:8-9), which reproach precipitates the prayer for death (3:11ff.). Like Tobit, her prayer reaches its climax with the petition for release through death from a sorrow brought on by insults (3:13). Sarah's protestation of innocence in her prayer brings out clearly what was evident in the testimony of Tobit earlier: this suffering has no sinful cause in the life of the sufferer, and its pain is made more intense by that fact.

These two tensions are at once bonded together in the proleptic passage which follows:

> The prayer of both of them was heard in the presence of the
> glory of God, so Raphael was sent to bring healing to them both,
> to scale off the films from Tobit's eyes and to give Sarah, daugh-
> ter of Raguel, as wife to Tobias, son of Tobit, and to bind up the
> evil demon Asmodeus, for it was Tobias' right to claim her. At
> that very moment, Tobit turned to go into his house and Sarah,
> daugther of Raguel, came down from her upper room. (3:16-17)

The storyteller did not leave much anxiety in the hearts of the
audience by this revelation! If the passage is not enough to
reassure the audience of the eventual outcome, the very name
of the angelic agent Raphael, "God heals," stands as a guarantee
that all will be accomplished. The suspense now rests in how
Raphael will accomplish his mission.

Preparing for the Journey

The storyteller may have brought the two tensions together
on one plane, but the protagonists are still far separated geographically. If the mutual resolution of their individual trials is to
be accomplished, the separateness of their situations must be
overcome. Since they are isolated in their problems, the next
stage of the narration must work to bring the two scenarios
together. The blending of the plots begins by reverting to the
story of Tobit. However, the first person narration is not
resumed since there are now factors at work which must be
known by the audience and which lie outside Tobit's ken.

Tobit is convinced of the efficacy of his prayer for death and
now arranges his affairs accordingly. The money held in safe
keeping at Rages in Media is remembered (4:1; cf. 1:14-15) and

Tobias is sent to collect it. The story of the journey to get the money will evolve into the main section of the narrative, with results that surprise all of the protagonists of the story (with the exception of Raphael). By following what appears to him as the inevitable way that God's destiny is heading, Tobit is unwittingly helping the real plan of God to be fulfilled.

The influence of wisdom thought on this book has already been mentioned, but it is nowhere more in evidence than in the speech of 4:3-21. This speech is more than an anxious parent's advice to an offspring ready to set off on an arduous journey: Tobit intends it as his farewell address to his son, at least in the realm of potentialities, as can be gleaned from the opening command to his son to give his father a decent burial and to honour his widowed mother (4:3-4).

As might well be expected, many of the "morals" of the story are represented in this speech. After a general exhortation to faithfulness in observing the commands of the Lord (4:5-6), there is an admonition to be generous in almsgiving (4:7-11) and to marry within the tribe (4:12-13). The more general wisdom advice that follows (4:14-21) re-echoes the admonition to almsgiving. In all of this, Tobit is only demanding that his son follow the pattern which he has set in his own life (1:3, 9-12, 17).

The journey into unknown lands necessitates a travelling companion, and here is where Raphael enters the story in human guise (5:4-6). The interview of Raphael (now Azarias) by Tobit gives the audience a tense moment or two, in fear that the angel will not be able to produce the appropriate pedigree (5:10-12), but Raphael comes through with flying colours. It seems that perhaps Tobit was not alone on his pilgrimages to Jerusalem after all — Raphael's assumed father and uncle went with him to the Temple (5:14). The travelling companions, Tobias and Raphael, set off, accompanied by the family dog (5:17).

As a family argument kindled the prayer which precipitated the solution (2:11-14), so a more minor scuffle marks the beginning of the long march toward the resolution of Tobit's problem:

> His mother Anna started crying and said to Tobit, "Why did you send away our little boy? Isn't he our support in his comings and goings with us? Don't pile up money on money and let our little boy become the sacrifice. For life given to us from the Lord, that is enough for us!" And Tobit said to her, "Don't complain, sister, he will come back safely and your very own eyes will see him. For a good angel will travel with him, and make his journey a success, and he will come safely home." So she stopped crying. (5:18-23)

Tobit has not revealed to Anna that he is, according to his reckoning, about to die; the audience might have noticed his careful choosing of words — as Anna has spoken of their life together (which Tobit thinks is drawing to a close), he speaks only of Tobias' safe return to his mother ('your very own eyes will see him'). As Tobit has kept something from his wife, the major secret of the story is kept from him; he even mentions it in comforting his beloved, 'a good angel will travel with him,' but it is just a metaphor for him, not a reality.

Solving Sarah's Plight

The central part of the book, chapters six to ten inclusive, deal with the resolution of the tension established by Sarah's affliction and prayer. This takes place in five movements, well captured by the later division into chapters:

1) the journey to Ecbatana (chapter six);
2) arranging the marriage (chapter seven);
3) the wedding night (chapter eight);
4) collecting the money (chapter nine);
5) departure for Nineveh (chapter ten).

As this division shows, the centre of the piece is the wedding night itself, narratively framed by business arrangements (for the marriage, despite the romanticism evident in Tobit, is still a business matter) and journeys. Paradoxically enough, while this section is loaded with all of the charm of the storyteller's art, the story temporarily puts some of its major concerns to one side until the story's conclusion.

The journey to Ecbatana (which of course is intended by Tobit and Tobias as a journey to Rages) is, like the passage in 3:16-17, full of foreshadowing. In the capture of the fish, the audience is informed about the means which Raphael will use to bring his healing mission to completeness. After Raphael has instructed Tobias to retain certain of the entrails of a fish they had caught, Tobias asks:

> 'Brother Azarias, what is the liver and the heart and the gall of the fish for?' And he said to him, 'The heart and the liver — if someone is bothered by a demon or an unclean spirit, these must be made to smoke before the man or woman, and they won't ever be bothered again. The gall, on the other hand — rub it on a person who has white films on his eyes and that person will be healed.' (6:6-8)

Nor does the prolepsis finish there, for coming into Ecbatana, Raphael informs Tobias that he is about to propose a marriage between his companion and Sarah; the emphasis in the announcement is on the legal right of Tobias to marry her (6:10-13).

For the first time, the audience has some intimation that the affairs in Ecbatana have not gone unreported among the Israelite exiles in Nineveh; Tobias has heard of these things, and expresses his fearful reservations to Raphael (6:14-15). But the angel's response reminds Tobit of his father's command (4:12ff.), the power of the smoke made from the heart and the liver of the fish, and the protection of God and of his plan.

> 'When you approach her, both of you must rise up and call upon the merciful God and he will save you and have mercy upon you. Don't be afraid, for she has been prepared for you from all eternity, so you will save her and she will go with you. And I suppose that she will bear you children.' (6:18)

Tobias responds with love and longing, perhaps bewildering when we consider that he has never met his beloved, but demonstrating within the terms of the story the absolutely complete response which he makes to the challenge.

In this dialogue between Tobias and Raphael, we receive a key into the problem of Sarah's suffering which we did not have before. Firstly, Tobias is correct in diagnosing the problem as demonic love (6:15) and is therefore justified in his caution. However, Raphael reminds him of the paternal exhortation which fulfils the law of Moses (6:12). Following that law will release the grip of evil and fulfil what the plan of God has intended all along.

The next section of the narrative (7:1-15) is the blending of fortunes: Sarah greets Tobias and Raphael; they are brought to the house, where they reveal their identity and the misfortune of Tobit's blindness. Once the welcoming feast is served, Tobias invites Raphael to negotiate the marriage, to be met once more with the history of Sarah's plight as a warning, but Tobias insists on the marriage. That this danger is being faced in accordance with the Torah is emphasised by a double mention (7:12, 13). Sarah shows by her tears that she is far from convinced that her disgrace is nearly finished (7:16).

The central part of this middle section (chapters seven to nine) follows a gentle chiasm which is not rigidly pressed upon the narration. It can be summarised as follows:

A. Arrival at the house of Raguel (7:1-7)

B. a Beginning of meal of welcome (7:8)
   b Business arrangement of marriage (7:9-14a)
   c Second mention of the meal (7:14b)
   b¹ Scene of domestic concern: Sarah and Edna (7:16-17)
   a¹ End of meal of welcome (8:1)

C. a End of danger: banishment of demon (8:2-3)
   b Prayer of Tobias and Sarah (8:4-8)
   c The wedding night (8:9-14)
   b¹ Prayer of Raguel (8:15-17)
   a¹ End of danger: filling in the grave (8:18)

B¹. a Beginning of wedding feast (8:19-9:4)
   b Business arrangement: collecting of money (9:5)
   c Second mention of feast (9:6)
   b¹ Scene of domestic concern: Tobit and Anna (10:1-7a)
   a¹ End of wedding feast (10:7b)

A¹. Departure from the house of Raguel (10:8-14)

According to the pattern of chiasm, the central event is

highlighted by balancing related events (or phrases or images) on each side. Here the (literally) central importance of the wedding night is brought out by framing it with prayers, signals that the danger is over, and especially two meals — one to arrange the marriage and one to celebrate its successful consummation. Setting out the chiasms involved as above might give the false impression that the text is extremely formalised in its structure; the author could have made tighter parallels in image and length of corresponding passages were formal structure the intention. But what we are presented with is a flowing narrative which uses chiastic balances for effect; such outlines simply help modern readers to see visually what ancient audiences would have perceived aurally.

Perhaps it is in this section that the author is most at home in the role of storyteller. The ease with which problems arise and comfort can be accepted (7:16-17) or resisted (10:1-7a), the pessimistic father-in-law's stealthy digging of a grave (8:9-12) and more casually filling it in(8:18), and the angelic handling of demonic pests in faraway Egypt (8:3) are all details which the storyteller has related in a way that the audience is sure to remember.

In the more important currents of the book, the narrative has reached a peak by bringing together the misfortune of Sarah and (more indirectly) the misfortune of Tobit. Because all parties concerned have acted in accordance with the Law of Moses (and the wisdom advice of Tobit), the blending of misfortunes has resulted in good fortune for one of the suffering characters; even without the prolepsis of 3:16-17, the audience would be in little doubt that Tobit's difficulties are about to be ended.

Solving Tobit's Plight

If it is true that return journeys always seem much shorter than the out-bound journey, it is never more true than in the Book of Tobit. Travelling from Ecbatana in Media to Nineveh in Assyria only takes a third of a verse (11:1)! The dog which marked the departure also marks the arrival (5:17, 11:4).

The story of the home-coming is told in such a way as to bring the blindness of Tobit into high relief. Tobit himself is kept unaware of what is happening, until the cure is effected. Note how the vocabulary which is chosen puts the spotlight on Tobit's affliction, both before and after the healing takes place:

> Anna sat *looking* down the road for her little boy. When she *perceived* that he was coming she said to his father, *"Look,* your son is coming and the man that travelled with him!"
>
> And Raphael said, "I know that your father will *open his eyes.* Then you yourself must smear the gall *into his eyes* and when they hurt he will rub them. *The white films* will fall away and *he will see you."*
>
> Anna ran on ahead and hugged her son tightly and said to him, *"I have seen you,* child. Now I can die in peace." And they both cried.
>
> Now Tobit started to go toward the door and *stumbled.* But his son ran to him and held his father and pressed the gall *to his father's eyes* saying, "Courage, father." As they began to hurt, he rubbed *his eyes,* and *the white films* peeled off from the corners *of his eyes.*
>
> And *seeing his son,* he hugged him tightly. He cried and said, "Blessed are you, O God, and blessed be your name forever! And blessed are all your holy angels! For you afflicted me and had mercy on me. *Look! I see Tobias my son!"* (11:5-14)

The healing of Tobias is now blended together in the narrative with the adventures of his son; only after his sight is restored does he learn of the marriage with Sarah (11:15). The rejoicing and praise of God for the recovery of his sight is dovetailed into the praise of God for the arrival of the bride into Tobit's home (11:16-18). A second wedding feast takes place, and Ahiqar takes his place in the rejoicing, as the audience would expect (11:19).

But all is not yet revealed. The audience is aware that the hidden reality of this adventure has yet to come to light, and the revelation occurs when Tobit tries to reimburse Raphael with characteristic generosity (12:1-5), thus resuming one of the great themes of the book.

Raphael's self-revelation takes the form of an extended discourse given to Tobit and Tobias privately (12:6-15). The introductory part of this discourse (12:6) focuses on the praise of God, giving thanks to him, and making his deeds known. Following on the last point, Raphael uses the label, 'It is good to conceal the secrets of a king, but good to reveal the works of God in glorious splendour' (12:7) to speak of the acceptability of almsgiving which 'delivers from death and cleanses from every sin, (12:9). Thus the happy ending of Tobit's tale is directly attributed to his past acts of mercy towards the afflicted. The third part of Raphael's discourse is also marked with the label of 12:7, this time to give a more detailed account of how he was sent by God in answer to the prayers of Tobit and Sarah, their efficacy assured by the kindly act of burying the dead (12:13). He then reveals his own identity. (12:15).

The initial reaction of father and son is shock, and Raphael reiterates his exhortation to praise, with an added explanation of how angels appear to eat(!), and the command to write all of this down in a book (12:20). With that, Raphael makes his exit from the story (12:21-22).

A *Third Resolution Revealed*

The story might well be expected to end at this juncture, imparting its moral lessons on almsgiving and marriage within one's people. However, the book goes on for some length, not in an artificial way, but in order to tie together some of the less evident threads which were used when the weaving began.

The double plot of Tobit's blindness and Sarah's demonic lover have been resolved very neatly. Even though the two resolutions were interdependent, the plots were somewhat nested so that Sarah's plight, made known to the audience after Tobit's blindness, is solved before Tobit's affliction. What the last two chapters will reveal is that the real application of this story is to be found in the outermost wrapping of all.

Modern audiences prefer the application of their narratives to be subtle, but not all audiences have shared that preference. The fables of Aesop eventually were given neatly phrased morals to bring out their meaning, and the same is true of some of the gospel parables (cf. Mk 4:13-20; Mt 13:36-43). Medieval stories sometimes had detailed analysis given after the story proper, revealing the entire story to be an allegory.

The Book of Tobit can hardly be described as an allegory, and considerable distortion would be required to make it into one. However, the last two chapters of the book point to the application of the story to particular events in the non-story world which might otherwise be lost on the audience. To the modern ear, such elements might sound extraneous and artificial; to the ancient audience, they unlocked the hidden meaning of the story as surely as Raphael's discourse revealed the hidden mysteries of God.

Tobit's canticle of praise (13:1-18) gives the first stage of this process. The text specifies that it was composed as a *written* prayer, thus not only one borne out of the experience of the one praying, but applying that lesson for a wider audience. As such, within the framework of the narrative, it is truly Tobit's own, it is truly a prayer, but it is didactic and (in the storyteller's perception of the term) prophetic.

The structure of this summarising psalm of praise and thanksgiving is not immediately obvious to the modern audience. It can appear to meander meaninglessly, beginning at point A and somehow arriving at point B, almost by accident. We have seen before in the Book of Tobit that the author can use a type of chiasm to structure the text and to highlight its meaning. Once more, we might represent this structure visually to observe what is happening in these significant words placed in the mouth of the main character:[4]

I. *Opening Praise of God*

a Blessing of God (13:1b)

  b God who humbles and exalts (13:2)

    c Command to praise in exile (13:3-4)

  b¹ Affliction for iniquities and promise of mercy (13:5-6)

a¹ Praise for the future action of God (13:7)

---

[4]An added warning might be given concerning the verse numbering which here follows that given in the Greek text. Throughout the Book of Tobit, this numbering is often at variance with that given in some translations. For instance, verse six in the Revised Standard Version represents verses six, seven and eight of the Greek text.

II. Tobit's Witness

a Tobit's own praise in exile (13:8a)

  b Exhortation to sinners to repentance and God's mercy

    (13:8b)

a¹ Tobit's exaltation of God (13:9)

III. The Destiny of Jerusalem

a The command to praise God in Jerusalem (13:10a)

  b Affliction and mercy for Jerusalem (13:10b-d)

    c Praise so that the Temple may be rebuilt (13:11)

      d Prayer for the exiled and afflicted (13:12)

        e The Gentiles come to worship in Jerusalem (13:13)

      d¹ Curse for Jerusalem's enemies and blessing for friends (13:14)

    c¹ Gathering of the exiles for the praise of God (13:15a)

  b¹ Blessing for mourners of Jerusalem's afflictions (13:15b- 16c)

a¹ Praise of God for Jerusalem gloriously rebuilt (13:16d-18)

The first section (13:1b-7) states Tobit's theme in general terms. He praises God who is the master of history and its fortunes, who humbles and exalts. He addresses his exiled compatriots, acknowledging that their present distress is the work of God; but the response should be to use the opportunity to make him known to the nations among whom the Israelites are scattered. As he has afflicted, so will he heal, if the proper response is made, and praise is again called for.

The second short section (13:8-9) is Tobit's own witness to his fellow exiles. After his own experience of knowing

God's mercy due to his previous acts of faithfulness (cf 12:11-14), Tobit invites sinners to come back to Yahweh and to experience his mercy. Although not explicitly referred to, this confession by Tobit of God's mercy towards the just is undoubtedly intended to be the lesson which he has learned through recent happenings in this story.

But there is still a greater application to be made, noticeable in the psalm by its very length: the pattern of affliction and mercy will also be seen in the fortunes of the holy city of Jerusalem itself (13:10-18).

This interest has not been consistently apparent throughout the book, and has even led some commentators to regard it as somewhat irrelevant. However, the concern with Jerusalem as the holy city has already shown itself in 1:4-7 (and to a lesser extent in 5:14). Jerusalem was far more to the Old Testament people than a capital city, as is apparent in these verses. Because it housed the Temple, it was the terrestrial home of the transcendent God; especially after the fall of the monarchy, the Temple became the geographical centrepiece of Israel's national and religious identity. Tobit is speaking in his prayer as one who has valued the significance of Jerusalem and its Temple, even when the majority of his kin had abandoned it.

But in the timing of Tobit's story, the Temple is still standing, relatively unthreatened. The storyteller is speaking of events which are still future to Tobit (thus casting him in the role of prophetic forecaster; the use of echoes from Is 54 and 60 adds to this image), but past to the time of the storyteller. The pattern of Tobit's experience, celebrated in the two previous sections of the psalm, is now given specific application to the historical experience of Jerusalem and its inhabitants.

This application is carried further by the conclusion of the story in 14:2-15. The prophetic verdict on Nineveh (attributed to Jonah in one recension of the story and to Nahum in the other) is cited as a warning to Tobias in his father's dying words (14:4a). The destruction of the Jerusalem Temple is explicitly referred to again (14:4b; cf 13:10), as is the mercy of God which will be manifest in the Temple's reconstruction, firstly as a somewhat inferior structure, and then as a glorious building which marks the eschatological age (14:5). Again, the prophetic witness is mentioned as a programmatic testimony to these events. This glorious reconstruction will bring about a conversion of the pagan nations, to the glory of Israel (14:6). Finally, Tobit instructs his son and grandchildren to leave Nineveh which is about to be destroyed (one recension cites a prophetic witness for this from Jonah). One last reference to Ahiqar (who apparently has endured his famous adventures in the time between 11:19 and 14:10-11) appears as a witness to the destruction of the wicked and the rewarding of the generous, blending together the destruction of Nineveh and Tobit's concern with the importance of almsgiving in a single object lesson.

Like Raphael, who only reveals himself at the end of his tale, the author of Tobit has only fully made his meaning clear in the final moments of the story. Certainly the book is concerned with the fortunes of the individual members of its audience, and advises them to ensure God's favour towards themselves by a faithful and merciful life. But even more, the Book of Tobit is a narrative contemplation of the fortunes of God's people, focused in Jerusalem and its Temple. The storyteller is not only attempting to shed light on the past destruction and restoration of the holy city, but showing that history is still moving on according to the patterns of God's mercy towards an eschatological Temple to which even the Gentiles will stream (14:5-7). This is a strain of thought which the New Testament uses in many places, none of which is more evident than Rev 21:9-27. The audience is thus encouraged to follow Tobit's example and be the responsive, faithful people who will interact with God's plan and bring the restoration to its glorious completion.

So the family of Tobit and Tobias is returned to Ecbatana in Media, a safe refuge from the destruction of Nineveh as well as the family home of Sarah. But there may be a still deeper significance to this choice of residential metropolis. According to Ezra 6:2-12, when the reconstruction of the Temple after the Judaean exile was brought into question, it was in Ecbatana that the record of its full royal authorisation was discovered, thus allowing the work to proceed. It might be simple coincidence. But it might also be the storyteller's way of leaving the family of the narrative's hero poised at a critical location for the tale's merger with the greater events of Israel's history, a reminder that every story finds a home within the magnificent saga of God and his people.

7

THE BOOK OF JUDITH: THE STRENGTH OF WEAKNESS

At its simplest, the story line in Judith is very similar to that of Esther. There are three basic steps in the movement of both plots. As in Esther, so too in Judith, the opening chapters build up into a mood of mounting suspense as the "Israelites" are increasingly pushed to the brink of defeat and disaster (chapters 1-7). Then, as all hope seems to vanish, they are delivered through the courage and steadfast loyalty of a woman called Judith (chapters 8-13). This astonishing victory gives rise to great moments of celebration and thanks-giving (chapters 14-16). But while the story of Judith echoes and develops many themes which are found in Esther, it is different on a number of points. Although tempting, it would be unfair to reduce Judith to a mere variation of the Esther tale. Even if both stories celebrate God's deliverance of his people through the courage and beauty of a woman, there is a world of difference in the atmosphere of the two narratives, in the characterisation of their heroines, and in the coherence of the respective plots. In short, we are confronted by the originality of two storytellers and their audiences, who, though separated geographically and by a couple of centuries, nevertheless share a common religious and cultural identity.

What it means to be Jewish

The tension in the story is built up by means of seven carefully linked steps (chapters 1-7)[1] that lead to Judith's dramatic and timely entrance (chapter 8). Her delayed entry into the movement of the story is deliberate and effective. At the point where the morale of the "sons of Israel" has reached its lowest point, when their collective sense of identity is most under threat (7:32), this beautiful and resourceful widow comes to rescue and reaffirm all that is good in being Israelite. Her very name, Judith, means "Jewess," and as the narrative progresses, it becomes increasingly clear that she is more than just a pious and courageous widow. She becomes the personification of the Jewish people, the epitome of their highest aspirations.

"Identity under threat and identity reaffirmed" could indeed feature as the subtitle to Judith. Although the opening paragraphs describe conflict and competition between the superpowers of Assyria and Media, and the audience is treated to a whole host of exotic-sounding and evocative placenames, it is not long before Israelite territories are

---

[1]These seven steps are as follows: 1. First Subplot and its Resolution (1:1-16). 2. Decree of Revenge is Proclaimed (2:1-20). 3. First Phase of the Revenge (2:21-3:10). 4. Israelite Response to the Crisis (4:1-15). 5. Holofernes' Reaction (5:1-24). 6. Achior's Fate (6:1-21). 7. Bethulia under siege (7:1-32).

unwillingly caught in the crossfire (1:7-10). Revenge is to be exacted upon them for their refusal to join forces with Nebuchadnezzar. This first subplot and its resolution (1:1-16) paves the way for the main conflict in the story, the deadlock between the almighty Assyrian forces and the tiny and apparently defenceless Israelite race. The lead-up to this deadlock is delicately timed to heighten suspense.

In grandiose and terrifying proportions, revenge is decreed against "the whole world" that refused to aid Nebuchadnezzar (2:1-20). Although the Israelites are not specifically named at this point, the audience knows full well that this bloodthirsty campaign against the whole western region will inevitably reach a climax when it meets up with this special people. The first phase of the revenge (2:21-3:10) consists of a terrifying recital of slaughter and defeat, as Holofernes' campaign meets with absolute success. Hearts are pounding as city after city falls, as inhabitants submit to the conqueror and as the emblems of their religious identities are crushed into the ground. There is a strategic and suspensive halt at the edge of Esdraelon, as Holofernes pitches camp "for a full month to replenish his supplies" (3:10).

This pause in the campaign's onward thrust gives the narrator time to attend to a question which by now must be foremost in the audience's mind: what can the Israelites do in the face of such unassailable aggression? Their response to the impending catastrophe takes place on two levels (4:1-15). They prepare for war, lay up food supplies, and defend the mountain passes. And at the same time the entire nation — men, women and children — gives itself over to prayer and fasting. As in Jonah, even the cattle don sackcloth (4:10)!

The fifth step in this build-up of fear and tension takes the audience back into the Assyrian camp to witness Holofernes' furious reaction as he learns of this unexpected resistance to his onward march (5:1-24). He seeks to establish the identity of this mountain folk: who are they, why are they different, why can they not be like all the other western peoples and give in without resistance? By means of these questions of Holofernes, and through the detailed responses given him by the Ammonite leader, Achior, the author skilfully evokes in the audience's consciousness a vivid sense of Israelite identity, reflected back to them on the lips of foreigners. Achior ends on the ominous and ironic note that it would be better to keep away from this nation if they are guiltless, for fear their Lord and God should protect them (5:21). The identity and hope for survival of this people is mysteriously linked with their God.

Achior is not thanked for his insights, however central and crucial to the story they may be. Instead he is scathingly reprimanded and peremptorily turned over to the Israelite camp, where he serves as a useful go-between to acquaint the leaders and all the people of what has just transpired at Holofernes' council (6:1-21). Although the report is not reassuring, Achior himself is received kindly.

And so the climax in this build-up of fear and panic is near at hand as the siege of the tiny town of Bethulia gets under way (7:1-32). The vast army of the Assyrian empire, reinforced by additional allies, moves forward to take the mountain passes and sweep majestically across Israelite territory. Details of military strategy serve to highlight the superiority of the invading troops, and further undermine what little confidence remains in Israelite hearts. The sources of water are captured. The Israelites are surrounded. Women, children and youths collapse with thirst. Conflict breaks out within their ranks. Uzziah, the chief man of the town, is urged to capitulate. He pleads for just five more days; perhaps God will answer their plea. The lowest point in the story is reached. There is conflict surrounding the town and there is conflict within. Small wonder that "the morale of the townsfolk was at lowest ebb" (7:32).

A Contrast in Identities

At this first major turning point in the story the narrator moves the action forward by a subtle contrast in identities. The people as a group have reached the point of losing hope. They want to submit rather than continue the attempt to actively withstand this overwhelming threat to their continued existence. It would be better to be alive as slaves, they argue, than to be wiped out. A note of empathy is stuck in the heart of each sensitive member of the audience, for this is a struggle that is played out many times on an individual level too.

Identity has to do with achieving a clear and consistent sense of who one is. A strong sense of identity provides a sense of inner solidity or security that enables a person to be an agent in life, to take initiative and make courageous decisions rather than to be a passive recipient of whatever the ebb and flow of circumstances may bring about. Judith's entry on the scene is perfectly timed. The people may be indecisive but she is courageous. They have begun to doubt God's protective care, but she is steadfast and single-minded.

They have tried to put limits on God's freedom to intervene, but she swiftly cuts through all this and in no uncertain terms tells them that "you must not try to lay down conditions where the purposes of the Lord our God are concerned" (8:16).

Once Judith enters the story, she remains on centre stage until the end. She is the chief human character, and her presence at each succeeding moment of the story is calculated to inspire confidence and a sense of identity. There is still, however, a lot of anxiety and suspense to be lived through. The Assyrian army is still as large and as terrifying as ever, and time is running out for the besieged and starving Israelites.

What was lacking in the people's response to the crisis Judith now more than adequately compensates for. In her address to the elders of the town (8:11-27), she inspires a new sense of hope and courage, based on a more authentic interpretation of what their relationship with God should be. Her speech is full of images that evoke a sense of true religious identity. God is not to be put to the test. Rather, patient trust in his good will to save should characterise the true Israelite. No other God but him may be acknowledged. His holy places, Temple and altar, must be protected at all costs. These present ordeals are not a form of vengeance from God, but a testing. With such words, Judith challenges the people to be true to their own deepest sense of identity, which is inextricably bound up with their God. Judith matches her words with action. Having highlighted the need for active resistance in place of passive surrender, she now indicates solemnly that she is "about to do something which will be handed down for generations to come, to the children of our nation" (8:32). Her announcement is full of suspense. The narrator is going to make maximum use of such suspense for this central part of the plot (chapters 8-13), which is now being set in motion. Secrecy about what she is going to do, the dramatic moment of her departure at midnight, and the scant time left to her before the deadline draws near (8:33-34), all these details deepen the sense of excitement and anticipation that is now going to increase until Judith has sucessfully accomplished her objective.

But first she prays (9:1-14), and her prayer contains a delicate balance between her unshakeable confidence that God is in complete control of his people's destiny and her awareness that she, a weak and humble servant, can co-operate with his plans to save her race. In her address to the elders she is strong and confident. In her prayer to God she acknowledges her weakness and looks to him for strength.

Judith's Plan

The main action at the heart of the plot falls into four graphic scenes. First of all Judith prepares to meet Holofernes (10:1-23). The theme of beauty lies at the heart of this elaborate preparation. The audience already knows that Judith is very beautiful (8:7), even if she has been clothed thus far in sackcloth and her widow's dress. Now they are invited to share in the delight that each group experiences as they discover just how beautiful she is. The elders of the town "were astounded by her beauty" (10:7); the advance units of the Assyrians "were enthralled at the sight of such a beautiful woman"(10:14); the crowd outside Holofernes' tent "marvelled at her beauty and marvelled at the Israelites because of her" (10:19); and finally when she is led inside the tent to come face to face with the dreaded general, "they were lost in wonderment at the beauty of her face" (10:23).

In her first encounter with Holofernes (11:1-12:9), Judith loses no time in setting her strategy in motion. She has come unarmed and apparently defenceless into the heart of the enemy camp. Her beauty and poise have gained her swift and unchallenged access to Holofernes. But it will soon become evident that she has other resources. The audience has already been heartened by her skill in oratory and her wisdom when she spoke to the Israelite elders (8:11-27). Now it will be charmed at the ease with which she can flatter Holofernes and speak directly to his pomposity, while at the same time, through subtle nuances and ambiguities, she does not compromise her own freedom and identity in the achievement of her goal. With his vanity thus appeased Holofernes is ready to do anything to retain such a charming source of gratification.

And so Judith has no difficulty in establishing a routine whereby her nightly excursions to the valley of Bethulia to pray and to wash at the spring take place with full authorisation and without raising any question. For the rest, she carefully avoids anything that would infringe on her religious identity — she refrains from eating non-kosher food and she keeps to her tent. How long can this routine last?

Because of Israelite panic, Judith has a five day limit (7:30). From the point of view of Holofernes' being captivated by her beauty she is operating against an even more precarious deadline. Three days go by. On the fourth day things begin to happen with an alarming speed. Holofernes cannot wait any longer, but prepares a special banquet exclusively for himself and his immediate staff, for the express purpose of "getting to know this woman better" (12:12). This second meeting of Judith with Holofernes will bring the plot to its dramatic climax (12:10-13:10a).

All the strands in the narrative thus far have been leading to this scene. Suspense is at its highest now. Judith's presence in the enemy camp has but one motive. Of this the audience and the Israelites back in Bethulia are fully aware. But they do not know if Judith can accomplish her mission, they do not even know how she plans to go about it. Everything depends on whether she can emerge unscathed and successful from this banquet.

The fact that Holofernes intends to take advantage of Judith does not come as a surprise to the audience, as they learn that "he had been watching out for an opportunity to seduce her ever since the day that he had first seen her" (12:16). They have been subtly prepared for this in the many allusions to her beauty and in the careful details of how she spent the first three days in the Assyrian camp. While she is intent on avoiding every kind of contamination with these foreigners, they are intent on devising ways of seeking intimacy with her. Judith's own skill in adroitly replying to Holofernes' compliments and tokens of esteem through flattering but highly ambiguous phrases contributes in no small way to the sharpening of this theme. Statements such as "Who am I to deny *my lord*? For I will speedily do what every pleases him, and doing this will be my delight to my dying day" (12:14), even if highly laudable and pious on the one level (if *lord* means Lord), are deliberately provocative as Holofernes interprets them, on another. Small wonder when he met with such apparent willingness to comply, and when she appeared before him in her finest adornments, that he became intoxicated, in the literal sense of the word, with the prospect of having his desire realised.

Holofernes' intoxication is the turning point in the banquet scene. As it precludes him from realising his desire, it ironically provides Judith with just the opportunity she needs for the realisation of hers. She acts swiftly and decisively. In the privacy of Holofernes' sleeping tent she beheads the enemy of her race with his own sword. Taking his head with her she rejoins her attendant. Then both women slip into their established routine of leaving the camp before dawn to pray.

All that remains now for the completion of this central part of the plot is the description of Judith's victorious return to Bethulia (13:10b-20). The release of tension on the successful completion of her excursion into the enemy camp is felt throughout the Israelite town. The suspense and anxiety of these last fearful days gives way to elation, joy, thanksgiving to God and celebration. The audience can sense the flurry and excitement as news spreads from group to group that Judith has not only returned safely but successfully. This scene of triumph ends with Uzziah's praise of Judith (13:18-20), the first of a series of hymns of praise that will highlight how Judith becomes the symbol of her people, greatly blessed and favoured by God.

The final section of Judith (chapters 14-16) allows the audience to savour all the delight that follows upon being suddenly freed from a terror that was threatening the very roots of existence. Judith, still in centre stage, gives brisk instructions for the completion of her strategy (14:1-5). Her role of inspiring confidence and a sense of identity remains with her to the end. Even Achior, the Ammonite leader, is so captivated by her integrity that he acknowledges the God of Israel and is incorporated into this people by circumcision (14:6-10).

Daybreak heralds reversal. It is now the Israelites who are on the offensive. Events follow one another in rapid succession as the plot culminates in the dramatic discovery that Holofernes has been decapitated in his bed by a woman's hand (14:14-18). The panic that grips the Assyrian army makes it easy for the Israelites to press home their advantage. Victory is assured as the fleeing enemy is overtaken by the now augumented Israelite forces.

News of the deliverance brings the highest dignitaries down from Jerusalem to gaze on the scene of the conquest (15:8), and to add their words of blessing and praise of Judith (15:9-10) to those already uttered by Uzziah (13:18-20) and Achior (14:7) respectively. Judith's own song of thanksgiving (16:2-17) comes as a fitting finale to this movement of exultation, as she attributes the success of her venture to the Lord Almighty. In these hymns of praise and thanksgiving Judith's identity becomes fused with that of her race, reaching epic proportions on the lips of the High Priest and Council of Elders:

> You are the exaltation of Jerusalem!
> You are the great pride of Israel!
> You are the highest boast of our nation! (15:9)

Her qualities of courage and unwavering trust in God become a wellspring from which a harassed and wavering nation can drink deeply, and find their true identity reaffirmed and reflected therein.

This brief overview of the Judith story line illustrates just how much the classical features of a good tale are present in this narrative. Drama, suspense, characters, fear, conflict, tension, resolution, decisive action, celebration — they are all there in a coherent and well worked out plot. But these are not the only ways in which the author of Judith has drawn on the rituals of storytelling. Some of the more striking devices include an abundant use of contrast, particularly in the delineation of the key characters, and a brilliant use of irony and ambiguity.

Use of Contrast

The story opens with extravagant descriptions of the wealth and power of both Assyrians and Medes and their respective rulers (1:1-4). This is followed by details concerning their military resources and prowess (1:5-16). The account of Nebuchadnezzar's dazzling victory over Arphaxad, and his preparations to take revenge on all those who refused to become his allies further emphasise the strength of this huge war machine. At the other end of the scale is the tiny Israelite people, just recently returned from exile (4:3), trying to defend itself against such impossible odds. On one side there is the fame and fear of the great city of Nineveh; on the other, the remote and unknown town of Bethulia. The leader of the enemy nation carries a dreaded name, Nebuchadnezzar. The centre of Israelite resistance has no such illustrious counterpart. Their *ad hoc* leader is not only a woman, she is a widow. This first series of contrasts focuses especially on the strength/weakness motif, capitalising on the folklorist theme of the weakness of widowhood.

The unassuming and diffident stance of the Israelites is highlighted all the more sharply by the pretentiousness of the Assyrian army. As the former urgently call on God for help they pray:

> O Lord, God of heaven, take note of their arrogance
> And have pity on the humiliation of our nation. (6:19)

Judith herself underscores this antithesis as she refers several times in her prayer to the pride and aggression of the Assyrians (9:7-10) and contrasts this strength with her own weakness (9:10,12).

The theme of Judith's *weakness* is a dominant one. What appears to be her weakness, often referred to as "a woman's hand" (9:10; 13:15; 16:6), or "a widow's hand" (9:9), becomes her strength. It is by means of her hand quite literally and by reason of the fact that she is a woman that she succeeds in the risk that she undertakes for her people's sake. What appears as Holofernes' strength, his arrogance and boasting, becomes the cause of his downfall.

At a still deeper level, however, the real contrast lies between the power of God and the arrogance of human beings. Judith is successful because it is the Lord, the God of the humble, who is working through her (9:11; 16:3,6). Her strength comes from her sense of identity, as a daughter of Israel. She can confront her wavering people and challenge them to a renewed vision of their future in spite of the present crisis, because of her deep-rooted faith in God. He is the one "who has designed the things that are now, and those that are to come" (9:5), the one "that the people of Israel has for sole protector" (9:14). When compared with the creative and provident power of God, the aggressive arrogance of the foe is exposed in its true colours.

As Judith's identity merges into that of her people, the storyteller calls forth an ancient theme in the collective consciousness of the audience. Israel's election to be God's special people was not because of any title of greatness (Deut 7:7). In fact it was the smallest of all peoples. Its sole claim to greatness in the eyes of the nations round about lay in the love and provident care bestowed on it by God (Deut 4:7, 7:8). Judith, as a widow, and as personifying the nation, is weak. Her strength, and that of her nation, can only come from absolute trust in the God of their ancestors. When this faith is strong and steady, God can work through his people to demonstrate where true values lie (9:14).

Another contrast that the narrator weaves into the story is that between innocence and guilt. The enemy is an aggressor. Israel did not seek to enter into this conflict. No reason is given for the initial confrontation between the two super-powers (1:5). It seems unfair that the victorious Nebuchad-nezzar should then turn about and seek to exact revenge on the western regions who, although they did not support him, did not oppose him either. Surely to have gained victory over the Medes should have satisfied the Assyrian's thirst for battle. But no! The offensive which Nebuchadnezzar pre-pares to advance against Israel and the other western regions who had ignored his summons to fight with him appears to be even bigger than the original one against the Medes. At least one gains this impression from the wealth of details and statistics supplied (2:5-20).

The theme of innocence/guilt is brought to the fore explicitly when Achior, the Ammonite leader, briefs Holofernes on the identity of this mountain folk. He suggests that it would be well to check first as to whether this people might have sinned against their God, before launching the attack (5:20). Otherwise, if they are guiltless, it would be most prudent to refrain from attack lest their Lord and God should protect them (5:21). The audience, already allied in sympathy with the innocent Israelites, has no difficulty in grasping the prophetic irony of Achior's warning. Succeeding events will show who is innocent and who is guilty.

Judith and Holofernes Narratively Compared

A study of contrast in the story's chief personalities further illustrates the storyteller's power to draw the audience into the movement of the plot. There are really only two main human characters in the narrative, Judith and Holofernes. All the lesser figures serve chiefly to pave the way for the critical interaction of these two. The audience can instinctively relate to each of them in diametrically opposing ways. In Judith they have a model of courage, faith and religious sensitivity. She typifies values deeply embedded in the audience's consciousness. and which are urgently needed in this crisis. In Holofernes, on the other hand, they can recognise and react against vainglory, pomposity and empty struggles for power. By sketching the contrast between these two figures in clear and simple strokes the narrator can help the audience interpret the more complicated conflicts that occur in their own lives.

They can be captivated by Judith's beauty so painstakingly described in 10:1-7, as she prepares to confront the enemy. At the same time they can revel in the futile attempts of Holofernes to gain mastery over this beauty for his own pleasure. They can marvel at Judith's skill and versatility in oratory. At one moment she can take the town leaders to task for their pusillanimity and attempts to manipulate God, and extract from them a spontaneous recognition of her wisdom (8:28-29) and piety (8:31). Then later, when face to face with Holofernes, she is able to adopt a different style. Undaunted in the heart of the enemy camp, her responses to the general are highly flattering but totally ambiguous. The subtlety of her flattery is completely lost on this vain tyrant, whose ambitions can be summed up in one word: domination. Unarmed and unprotected, not only is she in command of the situation, but in all her apparent flattery she never compromises on her own true identity.

Another vivid contrast in the two characters lies in the motif of godliness/ungodliness. Judith's piety is expressed in many ways. She is faithful to the memory of her dead husband, mourning him "for three years and four months" (8:4), with the traditional practices of fasting and sackcloth. Her prayer, after having addressed the elders and indicated that she was about to engage in some mysterious saving act, is a wellspring of sound theology and personal outpouring to a personal God (9:2-14). At the crucial moments in the unfolding of her plan she pauses first to pray that God's provident designs may be accomplished in the mission that lies before her (9:1; 10:8; 13:4-5,7,14,15), and at the end she bursts into a song of praise and thanksgiving (16:2-17) that brings together in poetic form the main themes of the story. Surrounded by her jubilant people, Judith, like a second Miriam (Ex 15:3), can extol her Lord and God, who has accomplished another "Exodus" from oppression and fear. Her song is a creative blend of old and new; of traditional psalmic elements of praise and acclaim interwoven with the particulars of this new deliverance.

Judith's godliness is also manifested through her concern to observe the dietary laws of her people. She takes care to bring kosher provisions for herself and her attendant (10:5), which she duly produces when invited to partake of Holofernes' food (12:2). At the very heart of her strategy lies a rhythm of prayer. On one level the nightly excursions to the spring serve the excellent purpose of establishing an innocent routine; at a deeper level, Judith uses these hours to "implore the Lord God of Israel to direct her in her plan to rescue the children of her people" (12:8).

Against such a background the godlessness of Holofernes stands out all the more clearly. In obedience to the command of his king, Holofernes sets out on a campaign of terror and revenge. Insensitive to all attempts to negotiate with him, he moves forward relentlessly leaving a trail of havoc and destruction behind him (2:22-3:8). All local shrines and forms of worship are demolished without exception, for all must acknowledge Nebuchadnezzar alone as a god (3:8). Such an arrogant ambition strikes at the root of Israelite existence.

If Holofernes is intent on eradicating all local forms of worship, Judith is characterised by a deep-rooted love and concern for the Temple and its liturgy. Her urgent prayer in

9:2-14 is uttered at the very hour when "in Jerusalem the evening incense was being offered in the Temple of God" (9:1). In that prayer her greatest fear is articulated around the possibility of Temple and altar being demolished (9:8 and 9:13). At the most crucial moment in the story, when she is alone in Holofernes' tent, she prays for success in what she is to do "for the exaltation of Jerusalem" (13:4). As the drama draws to an exultant end, she herself is hailed as "the exaltation of Jerusalem" by the highest authorities of that same city, and the last scene but one depicts a three month period of rejoicing "in Jerusalem, before the sanctuary, . . . and Judith remained with them" (16:18-20).

In short, Judith is resourceful and able to relate to different situations with different and appropriate responses. Holofernes only knows the power that comes from despotism, and in the end it becomes his undoing. The secret of Judith's personality lies in the harmony that rests deep within her, a harmony that enables her to face and overcome the insurmountable because of her vision of God and his enduring care for his people. There is no comparable mystery or source of strength in Holofernes, just one long campaign of arrogant and irrational brute force. Judith can hold in a delicate balance the tension between knowing her true relationship of dependence upon her Creator (9:5-6) and the need to act decisively and with courage within that context (13:4-7).

Judith is a strong character. Unlike Esther, she has no uncle masterminding her plan from the wings, and ready to step onto centre stage at the appropriate moment (Esth 8:9-15; 9:4,20). In the expanded Greek version of Esther, the heroine faints at the crucial moment of admission into the king's presence (D 6-8). Judith displays no such weakness when she gains entry into the enemy's camp. Not only is she able to meet Holofernes and his council with self-possession, but she enters into a long discourse, laden with ambiguity and irony.

Ironic Twists and Turns

Irony in all its forms, in fact, is a key tool that the narrator of Judith relies upon to stimulate audience participation and enjoyment. It is present in Achior's concluding statement to Holofernes, as this Ammonite leader provides a summary of Israelite history for the enquiring general:

> But if their nation is guiltless, let my lord refrain from action, lest their Lord and God defend them; we should then become a reproach before the whole world. (5:21)

The audience and narrator already know that Israel is innocent. The sequence of events to date shows clearly that what is planned to take place cannot but be an irrational act of aggrandisement. Achior's prophetic words contain the nucleus of the story, for the author's central contention is to show precisely that because Israel is innocent and because their Lord and God does indeed protect them, then no aggressor can stamp them out. Placed at this point in the story, how could an insensitive tyrant grasp the true import of Achior's concluding remarks? Their real purpose is to alert the audience.

The Assyrians' response to Achior contains irony of a different kind (5:23). Events will show just who is weak and powerless, and who will be swallowed up in one mouthful! As Holofernes himself reprimands Achior (6:2-9), and prepares to turn him over to the Israelites, his speech overflows with all kinds of unwitting double meanings. By a clever use of irony on the lips of Holofernes, the storyteller is subtly attuning the audience's ears to the possibilities that lie ahead when the tension of the narrative draws to the point of resolution. The callous Assyrian general may grandiosely claim "there is no god but Nebuchadnezzar" (6:2), and that "their God will certainly not deliver them" (6:3), but the audience's past experience of this God is exactly the opposite.

If Holofernes is totally unaware of the irony in his own rebuke of Achior, he is equally insensitive later on to the ambiguities that flow from Judith's mouth as she explains to him the purpose of her coming (11:5-19). While remaining true to her essential aim, she can flatter the vain general and his servants in such a way that they exclaim: "You are as beautiful as you are eloquent!" (11:21). How could Holofernes grasp the deeper implications, shared by Judith and the audience, of words such as *pragma* and *kurios*? When Judith speaks of her God actually sending her to do "things" (*pragmata*) with him which the world will be astonished at (11:16), she and the audience have one outcome in mind, Holofernes has another. When Judith assures him that "my lord (*kurios*) shall not fail in what he undertakes" (11:6), she and the audience know that it is the Lord who is in question, while Holofernes laps up the apparent compliment.

This irony and ambiguity is carried through into the scenes which follow. When Holofernes expresses concern that Judith's special food provisions might run out, she reassures him that the Lord will have used her to accomplish his plan before her provisions are finished! (12:4). And her reply to the invitation to attend Holofernes' special banquet is particularly effective in its double meaning. At one level it expresses Judith's identity in its most fundamental aspects: "Who am I to deny my Lord? For I will speedily do whatever pleases him, and doing this will be my delight to my dying day" (12:14). As interpreted by Holofernes' eunuch, however, it had a very different meaning, one calculated to lead Holofernes to the point of intoxication, and to disaster.

The Deeper Resonances

The success of Judith as a story-experiment, however, depends not merely on the presence of certain rituals or key features in the telling of the tale, but much more on the narrator's ability to draw all these elements together so that they speak to the deeper needs and aspirations of the people for whom the tale was created. When a story accurately portrays a vision of reality that strikes a note of authenticity in the hearts of its listeners, then it is true to its fundamental role.

In the case of Judith what are the values and vision of reality that the storyteller seeks to communicate by means of the narrative? The ending to the story provides a first clue. A happy ending has a reassuring function. No matter how great the conflict to be faced, no matter how insurmountable the obstacles, and no matter how unjustifed the attack in the first place, a certain attitude towards life and a certain set of values will win through in the end.

In the person of Judith many threads are drawn together. She is in a weak position, symbolised by her social status of widowhood. Yet she is strong and effective in her assessment of the crisis and in her ability to deal decisively with it. Her strength comes from her religious identity. This is portrayed very graphically in the superb contrast between the unarmed widow meeting face to face and fearlessly the mighty forces of the enemy. She takes them on single-handedly and defeats them. How can this be?

The audience is never left in any doubt as to the source of Judith's courage. Every move she makes is first checked out and tested in humble and earnest prayer. Her decisions are actively made in the unshakeable conviction that God is on the side of his oppressed people. Within the logic of the story the poles of the conflict may be exaggerated, but this is so in order to help the listeners recognise and grapple with these same challenges as they touch on each one's life experience. The first audiences who listened to this story could have been left in no doubt as to what it meant to be Jewish. When caught in the crossfire between stronger powers struggling for domination, and when one's own religious identity and very existence were under severe pressure, great courage was needed to be faithful to what could be called the visible signs of Judaism: prayer, dietary laws, ritual purity and above all, Temple worship. One needed far greater courage and strength of character, however, to be faithful to what constituted the inner strength of Jewish identity, a strong faith and trust in God that he would never abandon his faithful ones. The personality of Judith and the story that unfolds around her serve to encourage and reaffirm a people under such pressures.

Modern sensibilities may not be particularly attracted to the bloodthirsty elements in the story or to the gory details of Holofernes' death. As in the case of the Book of Esther, modern readers must enter into suspension of disbelief if they are to be "comfortable" with the images of violence and revenge that form the backdrop to the narrative. However one attempts to come to grips with these violent images, the essential conflict at the heart of Judith is one that continues to be played out on many "battlefields" and in succeeding ages. The imagery, the characters and the plot belong to a particular culture and era, and to their way of telling a story, but the underlying struggle to be faithful to one's true religious identity, no matter how crushing the odds or insidious the obstacles, belongs to every generation.

8

STORY AND DISCIPLESHIP

The discovery of the spiritual import of a biblical story, ideally, is a unified experience: we listen to the story, are swayed by its movement and artistry, and carry its vision away with us half-buried in the subconscious. The biblical story should affect us in the same way that a great play or well written novel does, through the involvement of the entire person in a learning process which is enchanting, captivating and enjoyable.

How To Hear Without Really Listening

Sometimes this unified experience happens; sometimes, but not often with biblical narratives. Their very centrality to our faith militates against their effective functioning as stories. If Lk 18:1-18 were read at the Eucharist every Sunday for a year, the proper response to the narrative for the type of story it is would still be a rare occurrence.

> He started telling them a parable about their need to keep praying always and never give up:
>
> "There was this judge in this town who didn't fear God and who didn't respect people.
>
> "There was a widow in that same town and she kept coming to him and saying, "Help me get justice from my opponent!" But he didn't want to for a long time.
>
> But then he said to himself, "Indeed, I *don't* fear God or respect people. But I will give this widow justice because she's a nuisance to me. Otherwise she will wear me out by forever coming to me."
>
> And the Lord said, "Listen to what the corrupt judge is saying. Won't God give justice to his chosen who keep calling to him day and night? Will he take his time with them? I tell you that he will give justice to them very soon. Nevertheless, when the Son of Man comes, will he find faithfulness on the earth?"

Taken in itself, the humour of the parable should be self-evident: the judge who is not only despicable, but who even admits to himself (and the audience) that he is despicable; the widow with no friends in high places or money with which to make discreet gifts; the final decision to make the right judgement for all of the wrong reasons. The humorous *coup de grace* is the comparison of this self-centred, resisting petty magistrate to the all-good, all-loving, ever generous God. But when we are listening to religious stories, we want something serious to take away with us. When we find humour or exaggeration or other storytelling techniques at work, we tend to see them as distractions rather than as part of the communicative process. We would be quite happy to stand out of respect as we listen to this parable, and acclaim it with alleluias; in some places it would be incensed and honoured with candles and processions and chants. The minister who read it would afterwards kiss the page it was printed on, as the hearers pronounce a final acclamation of praise. We are willing to award the passage every honour we can think of — with the exception of giving the story the very reaction it is begging for: a wry upturning of the lips at the least, or a chuckle from the very devout.

It would be valid to ask why we are so cold towards the charms of biblical stories. Modern Christians could offer a handful of excuses: the stories are so familiar to us; the culture that they use for a backdrop is too different from our own; maybe they lose something in translation.

But the biggest block to our appreciation of these stories is precisely in our accepting them as the Word of God. If our faith tells us that it is the voice of God speaking in these narratives, then there are several reasons for keeping the stories at arm's length:

Firstly, we like our revelation in neat, easily intelligible packages. Stories tend to be wild growths, rambling in a few different directions at once. The only good biblical story, from this point of view, is one that can have its message summarised in a few words; then we can memorise the phrase and throw the story away.

Secondly, some of the stories seem beneath God's dignity. The same people who like nothing better than the sordid affairs of television soap operas are the first to be scandalised by the earthiness of some biblical narratives. Then there is the matter of some of the parables! The wise bridesmaids of Mt 25:1-13 and the unjust steward of Lk 16:1-8 demonstrate a definite lack of Christian ideals. If the Lord *had* to tell such stories, we would have liked a parenthetical remark to show that he did not agree with the attitudes of the main characters. It would probably have suited us better if he would have omitted telling them altogether — after all, religious stories should present us with models for living and with people that we can look up to. And as for the tacit acceptance of war, assassination, power politics, the low status of women and other questionable elements to be found in many biblical stories. . . . definitely large parts of the biblical narratives could well be sent back to source for a considered rewriting!

Finally, and most importantly, if by some chance we really *do* hear these stories, we often do not like what they are saying. They challenge our quest for wealth and power, our sense of fair play, the facile optimism with which we can view the world around us. If we were to take them seriously, these stories would threaten civilisation as we know it. They shove us on at times, at other times pull us back; they are too forceful, too demanding. And we long for preachers and commentators who will reassure us that the stories don't *really* mean what we think they do; like children awakened into reality by a harsh noise, all we want is someone who will tell us that it is alright to go back to sleep.

Hearing Again, This Time With Feeling

If Christians are serious about taking the Scriptures as the Word of God, then they must be serious about listening to its challenges. Because story has a strange power to subvert its audience and to question all of the presuppositions which seem to give us security, really surrendering to biblical stories is an awesome step, a step defying completion.

The original audience definitely had the advantage of appreciating these narratives as the type of stories which the storytellers intended. They had few problems about laughing at the humour or being shocked by the ending. They had immediate understanding of the cultural setting — weren't they sitting in it themselves? — and details of the story did not provoke the moral inhibitions which our distance from the stories can raise in us. The first task of the modern audience, then, is to recapture this reaction of the original audiences as far as is possible, to appreciate the story as they did.

This goal is usually achieved with the help of biblical scholarship. A story may hinge on a cultural practice (such as the marriage customs in the Book of Ruth) or gain impact from shadings in vocabulary which are lost in translation (as in the Book of Jonah). Most lengthy biblical narratives will pose a dozen questions for us that we want to ask and a few more that we don't even realise we should be asking. The commentators are there to point out the rhetorical devices, to identify the historical allusions, to situate the narrative in its meaningful native environment. The wise use of commentaries and other writings about the Scriptures will help the modern reader to make that all-important step back across the temporal and linguistic barriers.

But after we begin to appreciate the biblical story as addressed to the ancient audience, the crucial step has yet to be taken: we must appreciate the narrative as a story for us, for our time, for our Church, for our faith. To a certain extent, the study of the story must be temporarily abandoned in favour of *listening* a second time. If the information gleaned from the world of scholarship can be submerged, at least partially, to let the magic of the story flow in and out of us — as it once did for the original hearers — then we have at least embarked on this crucial step of the process.

Plumbing the Depths

That hardly guarantees that we will always find narrative a satisfying way in which to receive God's message. We live in an instant world; we want diets that will ensure the loss of twenty pounds in as many days and cassettes that will have us speaking French in three weeks. In the matter of religious message, Christians have always wanted the precise formulation of dogma and moral imperatives in black and white. Sometimes this is easy to do, and the success of the Ten Commandments (as a policy statement, that is) shows that Scripture can provide this sort of thing from time to time. But often all we get are stories, and the stories do not always boil down to a condensed formulation of moral and dogmatic absolutes.

In fact, important stories require a lot of chewing. If someone close to us should die when we are absent, we want to hear the story fully and, though it is a painful story to hear, we will demand it be told to us more than once. We will ask for some detail that might have been omitted, some aspect that we may have missed. Then there are stories out of our experience which we tell again and again, sometimes even to ourselves. The narratives that we find in the Scriptures, historical, fictional or otherwise, demand the same sort of treatment. It is no accident that Luke, in the portrayal of Mary as the first disciple of the Way, describes her as one who stores all the events surrounding Jesus to ponder them in her heart (Lk 2:19,51).

On Passover night, as the Jewish family recounts the great story of liberation from Egypt, the telling is sparked by the questions of a child. After the questions are posed, the one leading the celebration says that there are different ways of asking the meaning of the night, one of which is to disassociate from the feast and to ask, "What is this ceremony *of yours?*" Needless to remark, the leader identifies this way of asking as a foolish and heedless question.

When we approach the biblical narratives, we can be equally foolish and heedless. Our very approach to them can be one of disassociation, presuming that these stories have very little to give us. We can adopt attitudes that would have done Marcion proud, effectively ripping out the Old Testament from the Bible in the smug awareness that the fulness of revelation has dawned for us in Jesus. How could the author of Esther or Tobit, unaware of such fundamental truths as the resurrection of the dead, have anything to say to us worth the effort involved in a meaningful exploration of these stories? How could the character of Ruth, so subserviently accepting of social mores which tied her marriage prospects to an inheritance of land, teach anything to the modern self-determining person? How can the story of Judith, spiced with a hint of sex and lashings of violence, add a single iota to the Christian vision?

At a superficial level, these questions have a point. There are no dogmas or moral imperatives posed in these stories that we do not find in abundance elsewhere. But it is not the function of narrative to give us wise adages suitable for memorisation. Stories are deeper than that; they are the gateways to mysteries. And that is probably why God is so fond of using them to communicate with us.

In the first chapter of this book, we adverted to the function of the audience generally referred to as the suspension of disbelief. Perhaps that phrase, excellent though it is, has too many implications of the rational mind; there is more at stake in hearing a story than rationality. Really listening to a story means more than letting go of a vague awareness that one is experiencing a fiction. It can mean momentarily abandoning prejudices, principles, one's entire perception of the universe. Listening to a story entails some degree of commitment to reassess reality from an entirely different standpoint; if at the end of the tale, we find our old perceptions more viable, we can always pick them up again. But there is danger, instinctively felt, that some stories will not allow us to do that, for they might present such a convincing picture that our old perceptions are damaged beyond repair. And that danger is most present in stories which we admit to be the Word of God.

Still, once we make that claim, we must take the chance. We take the chance by losing ourselves in the story, letting it lead us by the nose wherever it wants to go. Paradoxically, it is only by the loss of ourselves in the story that we discover how the story affects us, that we find ourselves as part of the story. We cannot approach the Book of Jonah or the Book of Ruth with the assumption that we will take from it a particular message. How far the story can lead us depends on where we are when we take it up. Today Jonah might challenge us with the universality of divine love, but tomorrow it might strike us between the eyes with an insight into our suffering. Because stories insist that we hand over to them our rational faculties (and more), the effect of a story upon our relationship with the Lord and with others cannot be predicted in the linear terms of a cause with a specified effect. The suitability of story as a means of divine communication can be appreciated precisely because of this power of narrative to move us along a variety of vectors, all of which wind their way toward the vision of faith and its consequences.

Stories Which Initiate Us Into Community

The biblical stories which we have investigated do more than address us as individuals; they impress upon us an awareness of the communal dimension of our existence within the embracing story of God's people.

At first glance, these five tales appear to have individuals as their centre and concern; we even call these books by the names of the individuals who are their main characters. But can this first impression be sustained throughout the reading? We find that Ruth's story merges into that of the dynasty through which God makes his people great, that Esther and Judith become the unexpected saviours of their people, that Jonah is painted as a warning caricature of Israelite jingoism, and that even the fortunes of Tobit are told as a pattern of God's dealings with his chosen nation, Certainly the individuals are important to these stories, but this importance. draws its existence from the relevance of these stories to the nation as a whole.

These stories impressed upon the original audiences that individual stories fit into a larger story, the story of God's plan working itself out in human lives. They warned their audiences not to see their own individual stories in isolation from that of the people. The importance of communal identity is stressed in Tobit, Judith and the Greek additions to Esther by stressing that these characters did not break the dietary laws, one constant reminder of the religious community of which they were all members; in Ruth and Tobit, it is the persistent observance of the traditions and customs of Israel which eventually brings a happy ending out of tragic beginnings. The message is simple: by being faithful to the ways of God's people, by being constant in one's self-identification with that people, one is assured of participation in God's triumphs for his people.

The communal aspect of these narratives is less palatable for us than for earlier audiences. Modern western humanity wants to find its identity as a matter of distinction from the crowd, not as part of a revered community, as the old jokes about young people all dressing the same in order to be different demonstrate. And Christian thought has also ventured down these roads. We have often become so preoccupied with the question of individual salvation that we have forgotten the more important fact that God calls us and sanctifies us and saves us *as a people.* No one becomes a disciple in isolation; it is through our interactions that faith is planted, grows and bears fruit.

It was a strong belief of the early Christians that they were part of the people who inherited the Old Testament stories, that they were "the Israel of God" (Gal 6:16). This was hardly a self-evident fact for those who saw physical descent as the key to being a member of Israel. But the element which assured the continuity between physical Israel and a Christianity drawn from all races and cultures was not a matter of genealogy, circumcision or laws of cleanliness; it was — as Paul so vigorously defends in his letters to the Romans and Galatians — a continuum of faith, beginning with its first expression in Abraham and stretching down through the ages to believers today. The people of God with which these stories invite us to identify is no longer restricted to those who share a common land, common descent, common language or common culture; the determining quality now is our faith relationship with God.

Since faith is the delineation of God's people, one might think that it would be easy enough to crystallise the content of faith; that way the individual could use the formulation to see if she, he or others could identify with the community of faith. This has of course been done many times, as the creeds and dogmatic declarations of the centuries testify. But might the circumspect verbal formulations and seeming completeness of creeds and canons be their central flaw? Perhaps it's time for a story.

> There was once a woman whose job required that she move far away from where she was raised, and the house into which she moved was miles away from the nearest town. Being a wise and sensible woman, she bought a map of the area before she moved.
>
> For the first few days, she hardly stirred without consulting the map. But then the map became less of a necessity for her. She began to discover little roads to beautiful places that the map didn't mention at all. Nor did the map tell her which butcher had the better meat or in which draper's it was more pleasant to shop. For that matter, the map didn't indicate

where the hill walks were for a Sunday afternoon, or the neighbours you could drop in on from time to time. It was a plain map with major roadways and placenames, and little more.

Whenever her friends or relatives were coming down to visit her for the first time, the woman would take out her map and sketch from it. She would post the copy to the people who were coming, and it would show them how to get to her house. But only when they had arrived could she share with them the wonders of her new home and its surroundings.

Maps are certainly useful, and many people find them an entertainment in themselves; but they are not the land. The map keeps only the more important features, rolls them flat from three to two dimensions, shrinks them at least ten thousandfold to present them at a glance. Creeds are the maps of faith; useful, but not to be confused with the real thing. Stories may not be as precise as creeds in their attempt to present faith, but at least they preserve a feeling of the rolling hills and the character of the villages. If faith is the hallmark of our religious community, the biblical stories let us know what we are letting ourselves in for.

In the first chapter, we identified stories as experiments in reality; in terms of the stories which we have examined in this volume, it is possible to make that statement more specific and to say that these stories are working models of faith, four positive and one (Jonah) negative. The faith in question is not the commitment to credal formulae (none of the central characters of these narratives would have got very far in reciting the creed along with modern Christians), but the commitment to God and to the divine plan and demand. The storytellers involved may have had little knowledge of our maps, but they knew what it was like to go up and down the roads.

Traditional societies (such as the Jewish and Christian communities of faith) constantly use stories to pass along their values with good reason: not only do the stories tell us what the values are, but they show that they can work. A receptive reading of Tobit should make us aware of God's generosity to us and of the need to be generous to others in response; the story of Judith should lead us to question human standards of strength and weakness. In this, we are being led willingly into a deeper appreciation of the values which the community of faith has judged central enough to enshrine in its narratives.

Although these stories were once addressed to audiences sitting attentively around the storyteller, we rarely experience them in their entirety in that setting today. We might hear bits and pieces in the liturgical assembly, but for the narrative in its vital unity, we are usually committed to a brief period of solitary confinement into which others can only enter as distractions. And yet, however we read these stories, the community is invoked, its invitation is extended and its values are portrayed. We hear ancient voices telling ancient tales, but also the living voice of God showing us what it means to be his people today.

Sharing the Inheritance

Among the many ministries evident in the people of God, certain ones are more obviously concerned with handing on the Christian vision to others. Parents, teachers and clergy are especially associated with this function in the modern western church. Considering all that we have said concerning the place of traditional narrative, it is no wonder that these are precisely the people who are most evidently the storytellers in the community of faith.

But a model which presumes that faith is normally received in childhood can be deceptive. It can encourage those who are not functioning as parents, teachers or preachers to see themselves simply as receivers. It can betray the complex network by which the faith of each is constantly enriched by the faith of others. The processes by which the vision of faith is communicated and enhanced will respect no stratifications among the people of God. That vision is too vast a panorama for any individual to see all at once; we all need to hear from time to time what is clear to someone else when it is occluded from our sight.

Perhaps we will leave much of the telling of these stories to parents and teachers and preachers, since they are generally the ones with the opportunity to tell such long and complex tales anyway. But it would be disastrous to think of the biblical tales as the property of these people rather than something which we all inherit equally. If the traditional story does not transform its hearers into its tellers, it has failed. Our telling may not be the skilled narration of a storyteller; it may be confined to fragmented insights we have taken from the story or passing allusions to the story itself, but even this sharing means that the story has become truly ours. The chances are that such sharing of biblical stories will come more from the New Testament than from the five short stories covered in this volume, but not to worry; Esther won't feel slighted and Jonah may even be relieved that his embarrassing adventures have gone unmentioned.

It is time for us to rediscover the power of stories in forming our Christianity. As individuals, we must learn to listen to these stories anew, with savouring and pondering and enjoyment. As members of the Christian community, we must see these stories as something to share, and listen to how the experience of other Christians interacts with these ancient narratives. And as a result, we will become sensitive to how God is still making stories, blending our lives and the lives of those around us into the all encompassing and ever continuing story of the people that he has called to be his own.

Appendix

THE HISTORICAL AND SOCIAL SETTING OF THE BOOKS

RUTH

The World the Author Depicts in the Story

This tale is set in the period of the Judges (c. 1200—1030 B.C.) and apart from the years spent sojourning across the Jordan in Moab, all the action takes place in and around Bethlehem of Judah. Whether the story is purely fictional or whether it may preserve elements of an ancient tradition based on fact is of little consequence to the story-experiment itself, even it it were possible to establish an historical nucleus. The world the author depicts is credibly that of the Judges, though with little difficulty it could be transposed to another historical period without affecting the main thrust of the story: the rewards that fidelity and trust bring. The only aspect that would suffer in such a transposition is the link with David, a most significant element in the final contours of the story. It is probably because of this davidic connection, which occurs in the last verses of the narration, as well as its setting in the Judges' period, that the book is now promoted to a place of honour before the first Book of Samuel, in which book David is first introduced. This promotion is attested to in the Septuagintal (c. 250 B.C.) order of books, and in modern translations. In the Hebrew Bible, however, Ruth is the first of the Five Scrolls, which form part of the third and final section of the Jewish Scriptures.

The story itself weaves its way through very ordinary human experiences, whether those of food shortage and bereavement, or of searching for a husband and the desire to have a family and home. It does so against a background of semi-nomadic and agrarian patterns (journeying about in search of food, harvesting, gleaning, threshing) and typical clan institutions (levirate marriage and redemption of family property) that evoke the atmosphere of the pre-monarchical days very successfully. The insecure plight of widowhood was a particularly harsh reality in the ancient world, one that required constant recommendation to people's generosity and good will. The unfolding of the widow's unfortunate condition in Ruth is very plausible as well as very touching.

The World of the Original Author and Audience

The story of Ruth is notoriously difficult to date. There are almost as many different proposals as there are commentators. These proposals range from early monarchical times

(10th century B.C.) down to late post-exilic (4th century B.C.). The situation becomes more complex if one isolates the davidic element (4:17b, 18-22) from the earlier layer, or the story proper (1:1-4:17a). For a long time Ruth was considered to be a post-exilic work, reflecting a reaction against the narrow and rigourist views prevailing after the reform of Ezra and Nehemiah (450—400 B.C.), particularly in relation to Israelites marrying non-Israelites. It was agreed accordingly, that if David's great-grandmother was a Moabitess of such high virtue, mixed marriages could not be all that harmful. And so the story was seen to contain a refreshing universalist outlook that could only be post-exilic. Such an approach might have some validity if the specifically davidic element could be shown to have been injected into the story at about this time.

More recently, however, the balance of opinion has placed Ruth back into pre-exilic times. There is no intrinsic reason why the "universalism" of Ruth cannot be late pre-exilic (c. 800—600 B.C.) or even earlier. The argument from language usage, that it reflects Aramaisms, and is consequently post-exilic, rests on slender presuppositions which imply that all influence from Aramaic must be late. Moreover, the existence of a superb piece of narration within the Second Book of Samuel (the Court Document, 2 Sam 9—20) or the wider unit of the so-called "Succession Narrative" (with the addition of 1 Kings 1—2) illustrates how alive and energetic the art of narration was in pre-exilic times.

ESTHER

The World the Author Depicts in the Story

The story of Esther unfolds against all the magnificence and intrigue of the Persian court. The setting is presented in lavish terms: King Ahasuerus (otherwise known as Xerxes I who reigned from 485—465 B.C.) is presented as a successful monarch who can entertain and feed his royal court and administrative staff for months on end. All the action takes place at Susa, the capital of the Persian Empire, and apart from the King, the rest of the personalities who stand at the centre of the narrative are unknown to us from any historical records, Persian or Jewish. Although many elements of the story are replete with the kinds of anachronisms and inexactitudes that also characterise the Book of Judith, the author of Esther displays considerable skill in describing the governmental organisation of the Persian Empire and the lay-out of the royal palace at Susa.

At the heart of the narrative lies the fear and uneasy existence of the Jewish Diaspora, reflected in one of the story's key building blocks: the plot to massacre "all the Jews, young and old, women and children" (3:13). Since we possess scant information about life and conditions in the Eastern Jewish Diaspora under the Persian domination in question (5th—3rd centuries B.C.) it is not possible to identify any specific persecution of Persian instigation directed against the Jews, which might have played an evocative role for author and audience. We can be reasonably certain, however, that the intense nationalist spirit which the

author succeeds in depicting throughout the story would
have been strong enough to antagonise any potentate or his
viziers afflicted with megalomania.

The author of Esther has created a world which has some
similarities with that of Judith: the instinct for survival under
threat of foreign anti-Jewish policy, the role of a Jewish
woman in saving the people from danger through her own
inner strength and piety, and the conviction (implicit in
Esther) that all will end well because God's providence is
guiding his people through every danger. Esther also contians
the narrative theme that success will come through knowing
how to co-operate, through subtle timing, with the superpower, while retaining one's own religious identity and inde-
pendence, rather than through total resistance as in Judith.

The World of the Original Author and Audience

There are two layers to the Book of Esther: the original
story in Hebrew, and the later Greek additions. These later
additions can best be explained by the popularity the story
enjoyed, their purpose being to give to the story a more
dominant religious note, and to make more explicit certain
elements which the Hebrew text left to the audience's imagination. It has often been pointed out that the author of the
Hebrew text avoids using the name of God and only does so
obliquely in 4:14, "rescue will come to the Jews *from another
place.*" By contrast the deuterocanonical Greek additions (six
in all, which exist in two divergent forms) abound in piety,
and it is not surprising to find that it is from these additions
that selections were made to represent Esther in the lection-

ary. These later additions, which were accepted as part of the total corpus of Scripture for the early Christian Church, provide an excellent example of the ongoing dialogue between storyteller and audience. In the Jewish world the Book of Esther is traditionally related to the feast of Purim, but the exact origin and extent of this connection is still a matter of debate.

It is difficult to identify a precise date for the composition of the book. The credible familiarity with Persian administration and frequent use of Persian loan-words would argue for a date in the later Persian period (5th—4th century B.C.). The desire to co-operate with the foreign ruling power without compromising their Jewish faith indicates a milieu much earlier than the Maccabean resistance period so evident in Judith (mid-second century B.C.). Although it is a blood-curdling tale (ending on the "happy" note that more than seventy-five thousand of their opponents were massacred in place of the Jews), it witnesses to the need the audience had of having their identity and separateness reaffirmed in the midst of very powerful foreign domination.

JONAH

The World the Author Depicts in the Story

From an historical point of view, the world depicted by the author in the opening verses of the Book of Jonah is highly credible. Assyria, with its capital in Nineveh, was the great source of terror for the ancient east in the time of

Jeroboam II of Israel (793—753 B.C.). Within thirty-one years of Jeroboam's death, the northern kingdom of Israel was to be destroyed by the ruthless and relentless expansion of the Assyrian Empire (722 B.C.). Small wonder that within the collective consciousness of Israel for centuries later, Assyria was to stand as the symbol of terror and oppression, bloodshed and deportation. In this context it is not a coincidence that some echoes of Assyrian might and power float to the surface in the stories of Judith, Tobit and Esther in their varying contexts.

However, from 1:3 onwards, the author feels free enough to dispense with any further serious effort to maintain credible links with the world of "history." The apparent reliability of the opening verses is increasingly undermined by what follows. The event that marks the turning point of the story — namely, the total and instantaneous conversion of the most godless nation imaginable in response to the preaching of a rather timid and reluctant Israelite prophet — is nowhere recorded in the annals of either country. Moreover, as excavations of the ancient city of Nineveh show, it would hardly have required three days to cross a city whose actual breadth cannot have been more than, at most, three or four miles! In fact, to look for logical (how can animals be converted?) and historical accuracy in this world created by the author would be to irretrievably spoil a masterpiece of immortal value.

The purpose of the author of Jonah is strictly other than to record for the archives an outstanding success of a recalcitrant and petulant prophet of Israel in confronting a mighty nation with the need to reform its lifestyle. But these historical allusions do have their part to play within the total movement of the story. A modern audience can enter more fully into that necessary suspension of disbelief when it can be more sensitively attuned to the evocative powers that such historical allusions had for the original audience.

The World of the Original Author and Audience

The bulk of scholarly opinion places this book firmly in the post-exilic period. The pre-exilic setting within the story is but a scaffolding, a device which the author uses to reach and to challenge certain contemporary attitudes of narrow nationalism and rigidity in the understanding of divine mercy and retribution. To be able to hold an audience through a story which describes the spectacular conversion of a dreaded enemy requires considerable distance in time for both storyteller and audience from the time when that same enemy was at the zenith of its power. To get an audience to the point of re-examining its own prejudices without feeling initially too threatened would also have required some distance in time from when the prophetic mission was in truth the conscience of Israel. It would have been unthinkable to have risked such a caricature of an Israelite prophet in the pre-exilic, exilic or early post-exilic times.

The Book of Jonah cannot be later than 200 B.C., for it was well established within the twelve minor prophets by this stage. In Sirach's praise of Israel's ancestors, the "Twelve Prophets" get honourable mention as such in Sir 49:10. The tolerant humanity and broad universalism of the Book of Jonah challenge an audience that has become inward-looking and narrow. Like the author of Job, the author of Jonah is making a bid for God's freedom to be God. Other nations, even pagans, can benefit and can be more open and flexible in their response to God's invitation than his own people.

Such an outlook fits in best in the fifth or fourth centuries B.C. when certain tensions were being experienced within the (by then) relatively secure post-exilic community. On the one hand, their experience of exile, their struggle to retain their identity and their renewed belief in being still the Lord's chosen people helped to reinforce a particularist outlook and a nationalism that shunned contact with all non-Jews. Struggling against such a narrow understanding of God's sovereignty and of Israel's true mission was a more universalist trend, already present in the great exilic prophets, but reaching its zenith in the drama of Job and the satire of Jonah.

On a broad basis, therefore, Jonah fits in comfortably as a brilliant but not bitter satire reflecting reactions to a brand of nationalism which flourished in the wake of the reorganisation of the post-exilic community by Ezra and Nehemiah (c. 450—400 B.C.).

TOBIT

The World the Author Depicts in the Story

If Ruth can be described as the story with the possibility of having closest links to an ancient tradition rooted in fact, Tobit is the story which is furthest from such a claim. With Jonah it shares an unfettered flight into the world of fantasy, but then moves into even wider orbits which introduce characters from the spirit world. Against an apparently informed background of deportation from the northern kingdom during Assyrian expansion in the eighth and seventh centuries B.C., the heroes of this story discover how God rewards those whose piety and fidelity to their religious traditions can withstand the pressures of having to live in hostile alien territory.

The opening verses of the story introduce the chief character after whom the book is named, replete with family tree and the circumstances in which he was deported to Nineveh during the reign of Shalmaneser V (726—722 B.C.). With a disarming simplicity the author has no difficulty in presenting Tobit, who is a model in adhering to the requirements of the Law both at home and in exile, as being on familiar and at times less than familiar terms with successive Assyrian monarchs. He is purchasing agent for Shalmaneser V, he has to flee the wrath of Sennacherib (704—681 B.C.) because of his persistence in burying those slain by this monarch, and eventually due to the intercession on his behalf by his nephew Ahiqar, he again regains favour with the next Assyrian king, Esarhaddon (680—669 B.C.) and is able to return to Nineveh, to continue a life of exemplary Jewish piety.

The story ends, as it began, with references to the current political scene. The author rounds off the story with details on the deathpangs of the Assyrian superpower, symbolised by the fall of Nineveh (c. 612 B.C.), and of how the remaining survivors of Tobit's family follow his advice and move to the safer regions of Ecbatana in Media.

As in the case of Judith and Esther, historical incongruities are not lacking. Among the more obvious ones are the omission of the reign of Sargon II (722—705 B.C.), who was son and direct successor to Shalmaneser V rather than Sennacherib (1:15), and the attibution to Shalmaneser of the deportation of upper Galilee (1:2) which was in reality the work of Tiglath-pileser (744—727 B.C.).

The World of the Original Author and Audience

That Tobit belongs to the late post-exilic period is beyond doubt. That it reflects the concerns of an author and audience in the Eastern diaspora is most likely, though a Palestinian background is not impossible, since the influence of foreign domination would have been keenly felt there at this time also.

Although its canonical form is the Greek text (which has been transmitted in three recensions), discoveries in Qumran have yielded fragments of three Aramaic texts of Tobit, as well as fragments from one Hebrew text. It remains to be proved whether its Semitic flavour rests on an Aramaic or Hebrew original. The Qumran discoveries indicate the popularity of this story and help to establish its date to about 200 B.C. The absence of any allusion to the Maccabean struggle which forms the backdrop of Judith confirms a date in the late third or early second century B.C. The ease with which an angelic figure with his own proper name can enter so smoothly into the vicissitudes of the story also points to a late date when the science of angelology/demonology was blossoming.

The story of Tobit provides an excellent entry into the best of traditional Jewish piety in the late post-exilic period.

While some of the story's elements are modelled on the patriarchal narratives, particularly on the Abraham-Sarah cycles in Gen 12 and 20 and the search for a bride for Isaac in Gen 24, the main thrust of Tobit reflects observances that came to the fore after the exile. Tobit can be admired and imitated by the audience for his pilgrimages to Jerusalem for the religious festivals, for almsgiving and feeding the hungry, for strict observances of dietary regulations, for burying the dead, for recourse to prayer, for instruction of his son in the pious traditions of his people, for observance of regulations for marriage within the tribe, for honesty in his dealings with others, and for his patient acceptance of trials and suffering. Tobit's own piety is reflected in the conduct of his son Tobias, as well as in the family of his future daughter-in-law in Ecbatana.

JUDITH

The World the Author Depicts in the Story

The opening paragraphs of the Book of Judith give the impression of being a precise factual account of an Assyrian king's encounter with a king of the Medes (Arphaxad), followed then by the revenge which the former (Nebuchadnezzar) sought to take on the Jews for refusing to join forces with him in his offensive against the coalition of the Medes. Not only is a date given for Nebuchadnezzar's declaration of war against Arphaxad, but an impressive list of allies and hoped-for allies is recited. Minute details are given with regard to the size of the wall fortifying Ecbatana, the Medes' stronghold, as well as military statistics for the infantry and cavalry of the attacking forces. Any attempt on the part of the historian to situate this king of Assyria (who bears a renowned Babylonian king's name) is doomed to failure!

The same can be said for many other details in Judith, which on face value might appear to be of either historical or geographical value in locating the story world. Bethulia, the little town in Israel which is central to the drama of the story, defies identification. Anachronisms abound: one of the most blatant is the reference in 4:3 to the return from exile (c. 539 B.C.) and subsequent reconstruction of the Temple at a time when Nineveh (which fell c. 612 B.C.) is presented as still standing (1:1; 2:21).

Whatever the purpose of the author of Judith, it certainly is not an historical one, in the sense of recounting actual past events. It is futile to try to anchor the world in which the author sets the story on any historical basis from within the story itself. The architect of this tale of epic proportions has used reminiscences from Israel's collective consciousness with a majestic and disconcerting freedom; the Book of Judith is clearly intended to be a fiction.

The World of the Original Author and Audience

Although the original work was probably written in Hebrew, the Book of Judith has come down to us in Greek. It was excluded from the Jewish canon at the end of the first Christian century precisely because it was not in circulation in Hebrew, an essential criterion for the acceptance of any biblical book into the authoritative Jewish Scriptures. Its deuterocanonical status points to a late date for its composition. Its religious message, that God delivers from the greatest of evils those whose faith and loyal courage remain steadfast, fits into the world of Daniel and the Maccabees. The happy outcome to the story would suggest that it was written not long after the incredible Maccabean success, when against all odds Judas Maccabeus and his freedom fighters dealt a resounding blow to the Seleucid ruler, Antiochus Epiphanus IV (175—164 B.C.) who had been attempting to persecute the Jews out of existence.

The author of this story quite clearly maintains an attitude of no compromise with Hellenistic mores. Judith is the epitome of Judaism in her piety, prayer and courageous action. The story seeks to reinforce in its audience the need to keep the flame of this resistance to hellenistic acculturation burning brightly. Hence the epic quality of the story. A date in the mid-second century B.C. (c. 150 B.C.) would seem to match well with the religious and political climate of the author's world.

Suggestions For Further Reading

On Narrative

Alter, Robert. *The Art of Biblical Narrative*. London: George Allen and Unwin, 1981.

Aristotle, *On the Art of Poetry*. (A readily available translation is to be found in *Classical Literary Criticism*, translated by T.S. Dorsch, Penguin Books, 1965.)

Crossan, John Dominic. *The Dark Interval: Towards a Theology of Story*. Niles, Illinois: Argus Communications, 1975.

Esslin, Martin. *An Anatomy of Drama*. London: Abacus, 1978.

Foulkes, A.P. *Literature and Propaganda*. London and New York: Methuen, 1983.

Riley, William. "Situating Biblical Narrative: Poetics and the Transmission of Community Values," *Proceedings of the Irish Biblical Association* 9 (1985).

Rimmon-Kenan, Shlomith. *Narrative Fiction: Contemporary Poetics.* London and New York: Methuen, 1983.

Scholes, Robert, and Kellogg, Robert. *The Nature of Narrative.* London: Oxford University Press, 1966.

Wilder, Amos N. "Story and Story-World," *Interpretation* 37 (1983), pp. 353-364.

On Ruth, Esther, Jonah, Tobit and Judith

Allen, Leslie C. *The Books of Joel, Obadiah, Jonah and Micah.* The New International Commentary on the Old Testament. London: Hodder and Stoughton/Grand Rapids: Eerdmans, 1976.

Berg, S.B. *The Book of Esther: Motifs, Themes and Structure.* Society of Biblical Literature Dissertation Series. Missoula: Scholars Press, 1979.

Campbell, E.F., Jr. *Ruth.* The Anchor Bible. New York: Doubleday, 1975.

Craghan, John. *Esther, Judith, Tobit, Jonah, Ruth.* Old Testament Message 16. Wilmington, Delaware: Michael Glazier, 1982.

Craven, Toni. "Artistry and Faith in the Book of Judith," *Semeia* 8 (1977), pp. 75-101.

Dancy. J.C. *The Shorter Books of the Apocrypha.* The Cambridge Bible Commentary. London: Cambridge University Press, 1972.

McCarthy, Carmel. "The Davidic Genealogy in the Book of Ruth," *Proceedings of the Irish Biblical Association* 9 (1985).

Moore, C.A. *Esther.* The Anchor Bible. New York: Doubleday, 1971.

Rauber, D.F. "Literary Values in the Bible, the Book of Ruth," *Journal of Biblical Literature* 89 (1970), pp. 27-37.

Sasson, J.M. *Ruth. A New Translation with a Philological Commentary and a Formalist-Folklorist Interpretation.* Baltimore and London: John Hopkins University Press, 1979.

Watts, John D. *The Books of Joel, Obadiah, Jonah, Nahum, Habakkuk and Zephaniah.* The Cambridge Bible Commentary. London: Cambridge University Press, 1975.

Subject Index

Biblical Index

Old Testament

New Testament